AUDUBON NATURE YEARBOOK 1988

AUDUBON NATURE

1988
YEARBOOK

LES LINE, EDITOR

 Grolier Books, New York

Distributed to the trade by Stackpole Books, Harrisburg, Pennsylvania

Published by

Grolier Books
800 North Pearl Street
Latham, NY 12204

Distributed to the trade by

Stackpole Books
Cameron and Kelker Streets
Harrisburg, PA 17105

Produced by Soderstrom Publishing Group Inc.
Book design by Nai Chang
Typography by Rochester Mono/Headliners

ISBN 1-55654-032-9
ISSN 0891-981X

Manufactured in the United States of America

CONTENTS

NATURAL PHENOMENA
V

WILD PLANTS AND MAN
VI

SPECIAL PLACES
VII

THE ARTIST AND NATURE
VIII

P R E F A C E

"What a great job you've got," I'm often told when introduced to people as *Audubon*'s editor, "traveling all over the world, visiting parks and wildlife preserves, and looking at nature." Well, they're half-right and half-wrong. I think mine is the best job on Earth, but not because it lets me jet to exciting places twelve months a year. It doesn't. Magazine editors are desk-bound creatures, dealing daily with manuscripts and layouts, deadlines and budgets. The thrills come vicariously, when my surrogates—authors and photographers and artists—return from their assignments, sometimes to remote lands, more often to locales far less exotic. Return with the words and pictures that can be molded into yet another issue of a magazine that hopefully will captivate two million readers. My job is not unlike the responsibility of a symphony orchestra conductor, who must fuse the sounds from a hundred individual instruments.

I've never been to India, for instance. My eyes in the subcontinent's wild places were Geoffrey Ward, author of an acclaimed biography of the young Franklin D. Roosevelt, and the photographers whose work illustrates his story, "Tiger in the Road!" This is writing so splendid that it was included in the anthology, *Best American Essays, 1987.* It is a wonderful account of a boy's coming of age in another world and another time, and of a repentant adult's return to the scene of his poaching exploits after an absence of thirty years. "City-bred and slowed down by polio," Geoff Ward had discovered the adventure stories of Colonel Jim Corbett, dispatcher of man-eating cats, on the long sea journey to India, where his father had a new post. Corbett's accounts "of growing up in the Indian forests were irresistible," Ward writes, "and I secretly resolved that I would somehow experience as much of it as I could myself." Ward's grown-up Indian companions "were initially willing to take me hunting mostly because I had access to a Jeep, then still a relatively rare thing in India. But after a time they seemed to take a genuinely avuncular interest in my having a good time." Such "good times" would be impossible in this enlightened day.

Since Kodak color film is next to impossible to obtain in India, the best pictures of its wildlife and parklands are taken by outsiders. Gunter Ziesler, a professional West German nature photographer, provided most of the scenes that illuminate Ward's manuscript; fellow countrymen Gertrud and Helmut Denzau, geophysicists whose passion is India—they have made thirteen trips there—and whose hobby is photography, added several stunning images.

I've spent uncountable hours lurking in camouflaged garb in the haunts of white-tailed deer, but with a recurved bow in hand, rather than a camera. Though I once won an archery trophy at YMCA camp, the deer population hasn't suffered from my trespass; meanwhile, I have enjoyed many frosty dawns watching the forest awaken and many orange-tinted evenings listening to the night creatures claim the woodland as their own. But Carl Sams sold his guns and bought a telephoto lens. Thus we have those extraordinary images that accompany Russ McKee's "A Contrarily Brainy Beast" and John Madson's "For Every Thing a Season."

The whitetail has always been a focal point in Carl Sams' life, although some would say that taking 30,000 photographs of one animal over a five-year span is an obsession. If so, it is a magnificent obsession. For his pictures are, quite simply, the finest ever taken of our All-American deer. They are remarkable because they capture the natural behavior of whitetails unperturbed by a human's presence. And unlike much wildlife photography, where the content of a shot comes first, the composition and use of lighting show an artist at work.

As an impressionable boy in northern Michigan, Carl Sams spent many a summer evening with his dad "shining" deer, watching does with their newborn fawns and bucks with their tender velvet-clad antlers. "Seeing these animals, learning about them, hunting them, became a passion for me," he remembers. In 1975, at twenty-three, Sams began to dabble in wildlife photography, but the deer seemed a lot farther away through a viewfinder than they had over a gunsight. Desperate, he attended a camera workshop taught by expert *Audubon* contributors, invested in better equipment, and with new knowledge and hardware headed for Kensington Metropolitan Park, a six-square-mile wild area west of Detroit.

Deer are abundant at Kensington but mostly invisible, for they are heavily hunted beyond the park's boundary. Carl Sams waited patiently for hours by deer trails, and one doe finally accepted his presence. When

Sams shook down some apples in an old orchard, she began to look forward to his visits. The next spring that doe had twin fawns, who followed their mother's lead and regarded Sams as just another woodland resident. And from year to year this pattern has been passed from generation to generation until the Kensington whitetails have become the best-photographed herd in America.

Japanese nature photographer Michio Hoshino has spent every summer in recent years on the trail of grizzlies, moose, and caribou in the wilderness of northern Alaska. But to capture the aurora borealis in its absolute glory, Hoshino camped for a month in midwinter in the Alaska Range. That's his lantern-lit tent on the opening page for "Natural Phenomena." Only on one night, however, were the northern lights ideal for photography. His exposures ranged from ten to thirty seconds with wide-open lenses on fast color film.

We tend to relate northern lights to bitter-cold winter nights, perhaps because the skies are so clear, the hours of darkness long, and the swirling canvas of color so vivid. Auroral fireworks, however, are not seasonal phenomena but are triggered by solar eruptions, as explained by Walter Sullivan, science editor of *The New York Times*, in "Curtains of Light, Horsemen of Night." The most spectacular display I could ever hope to witness was at midnight on a brilliantly moonlit night in September. My perspective: a window on a 747 flying at 37,000 feet over Alaska's Chugach Mountains en route from Tokyo to New York. For an even higher view, we thank NASA for Astronaut Robert F. Overmyer's rare photograph of the aurora australis, made from the space shuttle Challenger while speeding halfway between Australia and Antarctica.

In 1972, an offer that couldn't be refused took me to Ecuador for a two-week sail in the Galápagos archipelago aboard the schooner *Golden Cachalot,* launched in England in 1896 and now retired. Before our stop at Academy Bay, the main settlement in these volcanic equatorial isles, the ship's master, Richard Foster, showed me a selection of slides of Galápagos wildlife by a young woman whose home we would visit, and I was stunned. Tui De Roy was only eighteen years old; educated by her parents, who moved there from Belgium when she was two, Tui was fluent in four languages, an authority on Galápagos natural history from years of leisurely exploration, and an extraordinary photographer despite her limited equipment and a mind-boggling logistical handicap. She might not see her pictures for months

because exposed film had to be hand-carried to the United States by visiting tourists for processing, and the finished slides returned the same way! Tui soon had an *Audubon* cover and portfolio featuring her shots of giant tortoises, a new camera and lenses, and an assignment to photograph the red-billed tropicbird, the lovely "Longtail" in this yearbook.

"I remember the fresh green grass waving in the slight breeze under a brilliant blue sky, and in this grass stood a small bush with pale brown stems," wrote Bernd Heinrich in his book *In a Patch of Fireweed.* "On the stems were bright yellow flowers more beautiful than any I'd ever seen before. My urge to pick them was all-absorbing, and I forgot the black plume of smoke of an airplane falling from the skies, and I hardly heard the loud wailing of the sirens that slowly rose in pitch and then dropped, nor did I pay attention to the dull muffled thunder in the distance.

"As I was reaching for the flowers, Mamusha yanked on my arm. 'Komm, schnell, schnell!' There was a strange, serious look in her eyes. In an instant we'd entered through the steel door into a dark cavern underground where people sat like mummies along the cement walls. The thunder could still be heard. These are early memories, but they connect me even now to the present. I do not like forsythia."

Heinrich, today professor of zoology at the University of Vermont, was four years old at the end of World War II when his family fled its farm in what is now Poland just ahead of the Russian army. Then for several years, before coming to America, the Heinrichs lived off the land in a forest reserve outside Hamburg. From his father, an amateur biologist who had collected rare birds for museums around the world on expeditions to Southeast Asia, young Bernd inherited an intense curiosity about the natural world. This, naturally, led him to question whether the ravens in the snowbound forest around his cabin in Maine cooperate with each other in finding food. "Cooperation is common in the animal world, and it is often the key to survival in hostile environments." The answer will be found in "Ravens on My Mind."

These are only a few of the stories behind the stories in this second *Audubon Nature Yearbook.* I hope you will discover in these pages the same excitement I felt in reading these words, reviewing these photographs, for the first time.

Les Line

Les Line, Editor, *AUDUBON* Magazine

I
MOSTLY MAMMALS

TWO WEEKS IN A POLAR BEAR PRISON

TEXT AND PHOTOGRAPHY BY FRED BRUEMMER

Day 1—October 21st: The pilot waves, and the helicopter rises with a metallic roar, vanishing into the ash-gray void of gently falling snow. John Kroeger and I are alone on the cape. A broad, pebble-covered esker meanders across the cape from east to west, flanked on the north by shallow lagoons, already frozen, and on the south by marshy tundra ponds, hemmed by willow thickets. Two miles to the east, the cape ends in a crescentic, boulder-strewn spur that hooks out into the dark waters of Hudson Bay. Moist snow falls softly, evenly; our world is gray and silent.

A forty-five-foot tower stands on the esker, topped by a tiny hut, our home for the next two weeks. While we haul our provisions up, a polar bear shambles along the esker toward us. He walks slowly, ponderously. He stops, raises his elegant, triangular head; sniffs, weaving slightly from side to side; then shuffles on. He is a young male, high-rumped and low-shouldered, his long fur deep yellow in the gloomy evening light. He seems neither afraid nor aggressive, just intensely curious.

Polar bears assemble near this cape in early winter to wait for ice to form on Hudson Bay. The British explorer David Hanbury camped at this spot in 1898 because "polar bears were said to be numerous here..." It was early September and the bears had not yet come; he waited for ten days and did not see a single one.

Most polar bears of this region spend winter and spring on the ice of Hudson Bay hunting seals. Recent aerial surveys carried out by Thomas G. Smith of Canada's Arctic Biological Station show that Hudson Bay is home to about half a million ringed seals, the polar bears' principal prey.

In July the prevailing northerly winds drive the disintegrating ice, and the bears, toward the southwest coast of Hudson Bay.

Marooned on shore, the polar bears—the largest carnivorous land mammals, with the possible exception of the Kodiak bear—eat anything available: grasses, sedges, seaweed, carrion, berries. They raid eider colonies and eat the eggs. A few wander south as far as Moosonee at the head of James Bay, nearly on the latitude of London, England. Many just sleep, often in shallow pits scooped out on sandy ridges near the sea, living off the fat reserves accumulated during the bountiful hunts of winter and spring.

In fall the bears amble northward, bunching at capes like this, where they impatiently await the freeze-up that will enable them to move onto the seal-rich ice of Hudson Bay again. Surveys by Ian Stirling of the Canadian Wildlife Service, Canada's foremost authority on polar bears, indicate that about 600 bears mass along the 100-mile coastal stretch between the Nelson River south of us and the Churchill River to the north. It is the largest concentration of polar bears in the world.

Our hut sways gently. Beneath us in the dark a polar bear is leaning against the tower.

Day 2—October 22nd: Three bears sleep near our tower. All are young males, weighing between 250 and 400 pounds. As we clamber down the tower skeleton, they glance up with lazy indifference. One bear rises, yawns, stretches luxuriously, and comes slowly to investigate. He rears up directly beneath us, leans with his huge, sharp-clawed, fur-fringed paws against the tower for support, and looks at us with small, deep brown, slightly slanted eyes. In an odd way, it's a zoo in reverse. We are the captives, and the bears come from time to time to watch our antics.

Farther north Eskimos who once hunted polar bears with highly trained huskies now use deadly efficient snowmobiles, and most

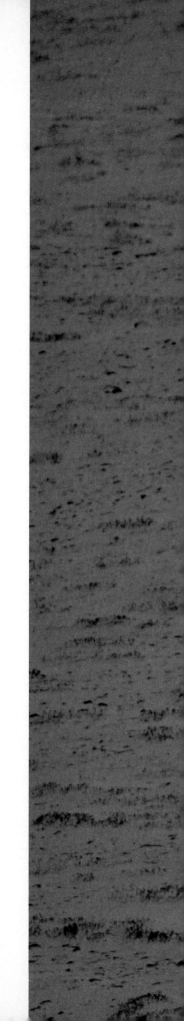

bears are wary. The quota for the entire Canadian Arctic is nearly 650 bears per year. Along this coast of Manitoba, the bears are protected and, as a rule, show little fear of man. But they are very cautious with each other.

Male polar bears, said the explorer–writer Peter Freuchen, are among "the loneliest creatures on Earth..." They always "keep some distance apart and never approach each other." Our bears not only meet, they spar and play and wrestle. But they do this only after proper introductions have been made. Initial encounters tend to be formal, ritualized, and tinged with mutual apprehension.

A new bear approaches across the dark, wind-polished ice of the lagoon. He stops. His long, sinuous neck sways back and forth, his coal-black nose twitches. His sense of smell is extremely acute. He lives in a world of smells; each breeze carries with it myriad messages. In spring, polar bears are able to detect "nunarjaks," the oval birth lairs of ringed seal pups, beneath three to six feet of hard, compacted Arctic snow.

Our bear trio dozes, but when the newcomer appears on the esker, they rise abruptly, worriedly. One walks toward the new male, and they begin a peculiar slow-motion, ursine pas de deux. They circle and sniff very slowly, heads held low, mouths closed, looking slightly past each other, signaling peaceful intent and mutual respect by subtle body movements, presumably evaluating by smell and sight each other's size, power, temper, and hierarchical standing. They halt and face each other, the hairs on neck and back slightly abristle, an outward sign of latent hostility and fear. They approach each other, the smaller bear, slow and submissive, taking the initiative. They sniff, dark noses touching, jaws agape. They paw and push, rise up on their hind feet and spar, lose their balance and, for one hilarious moment, stand locked in what looks like a passionate embrace. One topples and lies on his back, big paws pedaling in the air. The other, mouth wide open, throws himself on top. But they are very careful, very gentle, like two gigantic, shaggy puppies having a marvelous romp.

By nightfall, our coterie of bears **has** grown to twelve. All are young males, ranging in age from about three to eight years. All have been mutually "introduced," identified, and classified, and now they largely ignore each other. Most of the time they sleep.

Day 3—October 23rd: The weather continues to be vile. Yesterday it drizzled. Today an icy wind drives hard, granular snow across the land. It hisses past our hut and patters on the panes. A dark-gray gyrfalcon flies low along the esker, soars up, and lands on our hut. It is his lookout in this treeless land. Because gyrfalcons prey heavily on ptarmigan, governors of the Hudson's Bay Company at Churchill, reported the 18th Century explorer Samuel Hearne, used to "give a reward of a quart of brandy for each of their heads. Their flesh is always eaten by the Indians and sometimes by the English..." The ptarmigan lie low today. We hear them cackle in the willows, but none appear, and after a while the gyrfalcon flies off.

Toward noon a huge, emaciated bear comes to the tower. We call him Cassius; he has that lean and hungry look. He appears both evil and pathetic. Both ears are torn, and the left one is nearly missing; his eyes are bleary and bloodshot; his head and face are heavily scarred; his nose, broken in some past encounter, has healed askew, giving him a permanent leer; his fur is ragged and smeared with dirt. He walks all hunched up, as if he had a stomach ache. Perhaps he has, for he suffers from diarrhea and squirts out jets of liquid feces from time to time.

He walks directly toward us, hardly pausing to sniff. Our resident bears rise in alarm, circle the gaunt giant, but stay at a respectful distance. He ignores them. He shuffles straight to the tower, rears, reaches up as high as he can, and tries to hook John off his perch. He almost succeeds, for he is much taller than we thought, but John, despite his sixty-seven years, is as nimble as a squirrel and swings one rung higher. For a moment the great bear seems baffled. Then he begins to rock the tower rhythmically, whether in frustration or in the hope of dislodging us, we shall never know. He looks ancient and decrepit, yet his strength is awesome. The entire structure shakes and clatters; the steel guys alternately go slack and tauten with a crack.

After three minutes he stops and chews for a while on one of the girders—but not hard enough to damage his teeth—while frothy saliva oozes from his mouth. Then he sits, staring at us with a certain yearning. He is at least eleven feet long and, when fat, might weigh 1,200 pounds. In his present state he probably weighs barely 800 pounds. He hunkers down near the tower and falls asleep. The other bears keep well away from him.

Day 4—October 24th: Far out on the lagoon a bear tries to break the ice. He rears, pounds down with stiff front legs, and repeats this movement rapidly at least a dozen times. He

scrapes the shattered ice away and picks something from the water, perhaps sculpins, small bony fish common in these shallow lagoons, or maybe just a few fronds of seaweed. It seems a lot of effort for such a small reward.

Given the opportunity polar bears are voracious eaters. A large male can devour a hundred pounds of blubber at one meal. The high-calorie blubber is their favorite food. When hunting is good they eat only blubber and skin, and they do this, as Stirling has observed, "in a very exacting manner." He watched a bear in the high Arctic who, after killing a seal, was "carefully using its incisors like delicate clippers to remove only the fat from the carcass, leaving the meat." Successful bears leave a trail of bounty for Arctic foxes, who often follow them in winter and spring in hopes of leftovers, and for younger, less-experienced bears. But summer and fall are lean times for the land-bound bears. They sleep a lot, expending a minimum of energy.

Cassius the gaunt came again this morning to give the tower a good shake, but with less conviction and perseverance than yesterday. He has dug a shallow pit in a snowbank and sleeps in it. A young male ambles over in a friendly, inquisitive, diffident sort of way. Cassius wakes and gives him the evil eye. Slightly perturbed, the young bear pauses, sniffs, then very cautiously walks on. The great bear lunges from his pit and glissades across the hard snow like a gigantic penguin, on chin and chest and belly, forepaws pressed to his sides, rump high, hind paws pushing in unison. The young bear wheels and flees.

During the day a few more young males walk over to inspect the sleeping Cassius. They get a rude reception, and from then on all our bears leave the old grouch alone.

In the evening a huge bear arrives from the south and walks leisurely down the esker, immense power in slow motion, thick wads of muscles rippling beneath his immaculate, silver-glistening coat. He is not as long as Cassius but is round and sleek and must weigh close to a thousand pounds, a great male at or near his prime. Our entourage of younger males circles him with conspicuous caution and deference. Since he appears regal we call him Caesar.

He snuffles around the tower, licks the pebbles where we have poured down bacon fat with his long purplish tongue, then shuffles toward the snowbank where Cassius sleeps. The old bear gets up instantly. The hairs rise on his neck and back. He puffs out his upper lip and huffs and hisses menacingly, like a cornered cat. The newcomer halts, sniffs, then inches forward. The old bear champs loudly, rapidly; froth trickles from his muzzle. He seems to become more compact. It is the steely tension that precedes a lightning charge. But the great white male does not want to fight. He stands still, head slightly averted, and yawns ostentatiously, which seems to be a signal of appeasement. He slowly backs up and walks off with feigned indifference. Henceforth the two avoid each other.

Day 5—October 25th: The sun rises, a pale-orange disk over a land infinitely still and serene. A faint roseate blush suffuses the air

The tower on the esker, and a visitor. "It's a zoo in reverse. We are the captives, and the bears come from time to time to watch our antics."

13

and delicately tints the sea and ice and bears. In this pearly Monet light, a large flock of ptarmigan settles on the willows near the frozen pond and busily snips the buds. They look like bolls of cotton on the bare bushes.

A polar bear who slept nearby gets up and wanders over, not really hopeful but idly intrigued. The birds seem to ignore him. His walk becomes a stalk, cautious now and tense. At twenty feet he charges, an explosion of fantastic force, a blur of yellow across the ground. The ptarmigan cackle in alarm, clatter upward in a parabolic arc, and settle on bushes farther away. The bear lies down and falls asleep; then, beguiled by the smell of sizzling breakfast bacon, he gets up and ambles toward the tower. Dark clouds shift across the sun. Our world, so briefly luminous, is triste again and gray.

Our morning count is twenty-nine bears. This is not unusual. As many as forty-six bears have been seen at the cape at this time of year. Our presence and our meager gifts of food, particularly sardines—of which, for some reason, polar bears are inordinately fond—no doubt help to attract the bears. Feeding bears is strictly and rightly taboo in the North. In our case, Manitoba conservation officers do not really mind, for any bears we detain at the cape will not wander on to the town of Churchill, where their presence arouses some pride and, of course,

Two big males meet and an ursine pas de deux begins. They circle and sniff, heads held low. One bear topples on his back, paws pedaling in the air. "But they are very careful, very gentle, like two gigantic, shaggy puppies having a marvelous romp."

some anxiety but very little prejudice.

The attitude toward bears was vastly different when I first came to Churchill to study them in the 1960s with Charles Jonkel, then with the Canadian Wildlife Service and now with the University of Montana. Churchill was a boom town then, home to army, navy, and a plethora of government offices. Its population was nearly 6,000, and the annual fall invasion of bears was regarded as a threat that ought to be eliminated or, at best, as a nuisance.

But Churchill has changed. The military has gone, most offices are closed. The population has dwindled to about 800, but these are generally permanent residents, people who like to live in the North. Tourism has become important. Situated at the sea and on the tree line, with birds of coast and taiga and tundra, Churchill is a birdwatcher's paradise. Hotels are full in June and July. More than 1,000 white whales spend the summer near town, in the mouth of the Churchill River.

And fall brings the bears. Churchill now calls itself "The Polar Bear Capital of the World," and visitors come from all over North America and even from Europe and Japan to admire the bears. John guides a tour each fall to see "The Great White Bears." Tourists watch them from the safety of rented cars, from buses, or ideally from all-terrain vehicles that creep along the coast and seem to attract the curious bears rather than

frighten them. Town sentiment now is nearly solidly pro-bear. The hotspurs who used to chase the bears with snowmobiles, the killers who shot them from cars at the dump at night, the dumb kids who peppered them with .22s for kicks, have either left or changed their ways.

Our bears rest. Two young males who earlier wrestled and romped now share a snow pit and sleep entwined like lovers. The others lie scattered on snow patches some distance apart, rumps high, hind legs tucked under on either side, heads flat on the ground or, more often, pillowed on folded paws. They are light sleepers. A tiny sound, a whiff of food will rouse them.

At dusk an Arctic fox moseys down the esker, quick and nervy. Like a grayish shadow he slides silently past the sleeping bears, but most awake, glance up, then fall asleep again. The fox searches eagerly around the tower, but our bears have not left a smidgen; they lick the stones where food has fallen and eat the snow touched by a sardine. Disappointed, the fox hurries on and vanishes into the gloom.

Day 6—October 26th: Our bears are still with us. Some come, some go, but most of those we now know so well remain in the vicinity. Great Caesar sleeps nearby, and Cassius the grouch rarely stirs from his pit. Several bears, including Caesar, have tags in their ears, and I wonder whether Caesar is

"They paw and push, rise up on their hind feet and spar, lose their balance and, for one hilarious moment, stand locked in what looks like a passionate embrace."

15

A sow with two yearling cubs confronts a great male. "The mother rushes at the male and bites and claws. He hits her with a flailing paw. She retreats rapidly and, still growling and huffing, walks off with her cubs."

one of the youngsters I helped to tag back in the 1960s.

The polar bear's realm is immense—five million square miles of circumpolar land and frozen sea. In the vivid imagery of their poems, Eskimos call the polar bear "pihoqahiaq," the ever-wandering one. Once, it was thought that polar bears roamed the top of the world from continent to continent, eternal nomads of the North. They do turn up in the remotest places.

In May 1926 the explorers Lincoln Ells-worth and Roald Amundsen crossed the frozen Arctic Ocean in the airship *Norge* from Spitsbergen to Alaska. Near the "Ice Pole" (86°N, 157°W), "the most inaccessible spot in the Arctic regions," they saw "one lone polar bear track." In 1961, when I traversed the ice cap of Spitsbergen with a British expedition, we came across polar bear tracks at the base of Newtontoppen, the highest mountain of the Spitsbergen Archipelago.

But the recapture of tagged bears and recent genetic and morphological studies indicate that most polar bears belong to geographically discrete populations. Bears tagged near Churchill are caught or observed in the same area in subsequent years, and some of the bears we now watch will, no doubt, be here again next fall.

The younger bears often play together, but they avoid the three great males (the third arrived this morning). Caesar has tried repeatedly to make friends with some of the subadults, bears of between 250 and 500 pounds. He walks toward them, slow, friendly, inquisitive, but the smaller bears are tense and apprehensive. They back off and sometimes run.

As soon as food is involved, though, this respect for rank and hierarchy declines. We scatter lunch. Three young bears come immediately and so, a bit behind, does Caesar. The small bears growl but do not budge. They pick and lick the bits of stew and noodles from the rocks. The big bear does not

charge or even threaten. He eases sideways and keeps pushing in until his muzzle is only inches from the nearest bear who, still growling and very reluctant, slowly begins to yield. Prior presence at a source of food seems to confer some rights. When the young bears are first, the big males muscle in but are cautious and circumspect, and the meal is usually shared, albeit in a rather tense atmosphere. When a big bear is first and a small bear comes near, the big one growls a warning and, if this is ignored, may turn on the intruder with a roar and chase him away.

Day 7—October 27th: Until today, all bears at the cape have been males. We have seen females with cubs only in the distance. They shun the cape, for males may kill cubs and have been known to kill the mother as well. Since males usually cluster at the capes, females with cubs tend to wait for freeze-up farther inland.

In the winter of 1969–70, Charles Jonkel discovered a major polar bear denning area in the forest and lake region between the Broad and Nelson rivers to the south of us. Stirling estimates that about 80 females den in Manitoba each winter and roughly 150 cubs are born, usually in December or January.

The cub that now follows a female along the esker is ten or eleven months old, a chubby miniature edition of its massive mother. She is extremely cautious. She walks a bit, with the cub directly behind her or close to her side, stops often, and sniffs. She came from upwind but now has circled to leeward to test the breeze, to take warning from the multitude of messages it carries.

Our resident bears sleep within a few hundred yards of the tower, yellowish humps upon patches of snow. If we scatter food, they may trot up; if threatened by a big male, they may jump aside and trot off. At all other times they move slowly and deliberately. (Because of the polar bear's rolling, ponderous gait, 19th Century whalers called it the "farmer.") It should be easy for us to keep track of all bears in the vicinity. Yet they have a disconcerting ability to appear and disappear unexpectedly. Ten minutes ago, I counted fourteen bears near us. Then I watched the female and cub. Now I count again and two are gone, and no amount of searching reveals their whereabouts. For all their bulk and seeming slowness, the bears can move with amazing speed and stealth. They pad along in utter silence, vanish behind a knoll, lie still, and blend with land and snow.

The female and her cub come closer, the mother worried, the cub intensely curious. A young male slowly ambles toward them. The female "talks" to her cub in low grunts. The cub hides behind her but peeks around her broad rump from time to time.

As the young male draws near, the female becomes increasingly hostile: ears flat against

her head, hairs slightly raised, head lowered, staring directly at the advancing bear. The male is inquisitive but cautious, and signals "peace" as explicitly as he can with every nuance of body posture and movement. He reaches her. They sniff, the female tense and defensive, the male cautiously curious and friendly. The female growls, and the young bear backs off and walks away. The female and cub lie down, but she is nervous. In the evening they leave. Near a little bush, the cub smells something interesting and pauses to poke and sniff. The female walks on, then turns and calls the cub, which obediently joins her.

Day 8–9—October 28th–29th: It storms. Our tower sways and clanks and groans; the wind wails eerily in the guys and girders. We seem suspended in a swirling world all white; at times we cannot even see the ground. Five bears sleep near the tower, oblivious, it seems, to the icy gusts that reach 70 mph and to the stinging, wind-whipped snow. Triangular drifts build up against the bears; they sleep on blissfully. Their thick layer of insulating blubber and dense, oily wool covered by a long, shaggy coat of guard hairs make adult polar bears virtually impervious to the worst Arctic weather.

Only the cubs seem singularly ill-prepared for their midwinter birth: They weigh barely one and a half pounds and are blind, deaf, and naked. In November the pregnant female digs a den in a deep snowdrift, usually in an area that has been used by denning polar bears for untold generations and, most likely, not far from the place where she herself was born. The den may be a simple oval, five to ten feet long and about three feet high, or it may have several chambers. As in Eskimo igloos the entrance tunnel slopes upward so warm air will not escape, and drifting snow usually seals it. Since snow is an excellent insulator, the temperature inside the den may be 40 degrees warmer than the temperature outside. The cubs snuggle into their mother's deep-pile fur and suckle her fat-rich milk. She reclines on her back and cradles the cubs upon her chest with her massive furry paws. When the cubs are cold they cry, and the mother curls up protectively and hugs them closer. The cubs grow quickly. At two months they weigh about eleven pounds, are densely furred, and begin to explore their gloomy world.

The Canadian scientist Richard Harington opened a den on Southampton Island in northern Hudson Bay. "A glistening black eye and twitching muzzle were instantly applied to the aperture by the mother bear.

While she paced the den floor beneath us, uttering peevish grunts, we were just able to discern her two young cubs huddled against the far wall of their snow house." When they emerge from the darkness of their den into the dazzling glitter of the Arctic in late March, the cubs weigh a chubby twenty pounds.

During brief lulls in the storm we try to spot the other bears. It is nearly impossible; they have become as one with the land. Old Cassius, buried in his pit, is now just a slight hump on the snowbank, visible to us only because we know the exact spot where he sleeps.

Toward evening of the second day, the storm abates. Here and there, like mounds of snow come to life, polar bears rise and shake themselves. They seem itchy after their long rest. They roll and rub in the snow, twisting and turning with sensuous pleasure, great paws wagging limply in the air. One backs into a willow bush to rub his rump, another slides back and forth across the stunted willows to scratch his belly. Four young males have left the cape; two newcomers, also young males, have joined us. They make the rounds and "introduce" themselves, sniffing the bigger males from a respectful distance, pawing and romping with their peers.

At night the northern lights are spectacular. Constantly changing streamers and whorls and curtains of greenish-white shift and sway across the sky, silent and superb. They flare and flow in eerie splendor against the velvet-black of night, changing to deep violet and back to pale green, the silent dance of spectral fire. They are, say Eskimo legends, the souls of the dead at play.

Day 10—October 30th: It is a glorious day, our first and last. The air is as cool and clear as chilled champagne, the sky a gentle blue, the snow and ice aglitter. Near the coast a red fox pesters a bear. It is a silly game and seems a trifle risky, but the fox keeps it up for more than half an hour.

The bear, a young male, sleeps. The fox traipses past. The bear charges, not really in earnest but in a sort of rolling trot. The fox skips nimbly away. The bear lies down, the fox comes mincing back. The bear looks but does not charge. The fox sashays past just feet away. Up goes the bear, a lumbering lummox, and off goes the fox with a lithe pirouette. The bear lies down, but the fox will not give up. Closer and closer he comes, enticing the bear to charge. And the bear does charge, again and again, but finally he has had enough and walks away. The fox tries his wiles on another bear, a big male who

charges once, then goes to sleep and will not budge. The fox makes a few more passes, is completely ignored, and trots off.

In the morning, a female with two cubs arrives. They are close to two years old, a male nearly as big as the mother, though not as massive and heavy, and a smaller female sibling. The male is brash and disobedient. He often strays far from the mother and does not always come when called. The little female is meeker and usually remains close to her mother.

This trio is much more venturesome than the timid female with her yearling cub who visited the esker three days ago. Although we now have about a dozen males in the vicinity of the tower, the new arrivals march right up. The female is cautious but seems little worried about the young males, who weigh as much as she does—about 500 pounds. When she lets them approach or approaches them, they sniff and paw and push in friendly play, though never for long.

But when great Caesar idles up, the female instantly becomes all fear and fury. She huffs an urgent warning, and her cubs come at once; the female huddles behind her, the male stands by her side. The big bear is cautious but persistent. He keeps coming closer. When he is ten yards away, the mother charges with a roar. The female cub remains behind, the male charges with his mother but does not actually tackle or even touch the great bear. The mother rushes at the male and bites and claws. They rear up for an instant and he hits her with a flailing paw. She drops aside, retreats rapidly and, still growling and huffing, walks off with her cubs. The big bear stands immobile and watches them go. Although the fight looked fierce, neither bear is injured, and female and cubs remain near the tower.

The female has one more fight with a big bear and several minor skirmishes with smaller males, the latter invariably provoked by the brazen behavior of the male cub. He walks toward a young male, moans loudly to incite his mother, and charges the male, uttering at the same time the plaintive wail of a frightened cub. Instantly enraged, the mother charges and puts the inoffensive male to rout. It is a blatant ploy, but the male cub uses it time after time, and the mother always rushes to his defense.

The sun sets. The ice on the lagoon glows in somber bronze split by a path of silver. In this line of searing white stands a lone bear, a massive dark shape haloed in gold.

Day 11-14—October 31st-November 3rd: We've had the single magnificent day of our entire stay. It is gloomy now and gray. It snows a bit and blows. The bears begin to leave.

Some wander to the very tip of the cape. Others just amble away. Even Cassius, who has slept nearby for eleven days, shuffles off, looking very old and ailing. The plane arrives and bounces along the esker, chasing the remaining bears away. Our captivity is over; for the first time in fourteen days we come to earth again.

On November 9th, slob ice begins to form along the coast. By the 13th it has congealed, and ice stretches far out to sea. By November 15th nearly all of the bears have left the land to hunt again for seals on the ice of Hudson Bay.

"The female and cub lie down, but she is nervous. In the evening they leave. Near a little bush, the cub smells something interesting and pauses to poke and sniff. The female walks on, then turns and calls the cub, which obediently joins her."

THE EARS OF LEPUS CALIFORNICUS

TEXT AND PHOTOGRAPH BY RICHARD W. CLARK

I chanced to be visited by some Shawnee Indians who were in the area on a hunting expedition. They were highly astonished and pleased with my drawings, which I showed them while trying to explain what animals I wanted. I made a hasty sketch of a hare with immensely long ears, at which I pointed with an approving nod, and then made another sketch smaller and with smaller ears, at which last I shook my head and made wry faces. The Indians laughed, and in a day or two I had a beautiful specimen of the Black-tailed Rabbit brought to me.

—*John James Audubon*

It's not surprising that Audubon emphasized the ears in his description of *Lepus californicus,* the black-tailed jackrabbit. These auditory appendages grow to six or seven inches in length on a body only three times as long. During the Mexican War, our troops were equally impressed with the mammal's ears and called it the "Jackass Rabbit."

The jackrabbit is not a true rabbit, but a hare. Rabbits, such as the cottontail, belong to the genus *Sylvilagus,* have shorter ears and shorter hind legs than jacks, and give birth to altricial young—born blind, furless, and helpless. Hares, on the other hand, enter the world with their eyes open, fully furred, and able to hop away from danger shortly after birth.

A jackrabbit's ears, or pinnae, serve it well for survival in its western habitat. Typically, it holds them erect, listening for any sounds that could mean danger. The blacktail can rotate each of its ears independently to pinpoint a threatening sound's source. Should the enemy come closer, the jack will crouch motionless and lay its ears flat against its back, thus becoming less conspicuous.

The fuzzy, translucent pinnae account for about 19 percent of a jackrabbit's body surface area. Their pinkish-orange color when backlit is caused by the vast network of blood vessels running through them, forming a specialized section of the circulatory system —an adaptation that serves as a cooling system. Blood flow is controlled at the base of the ears, and when a jack is overheated it can pump blood through them, thus dissipating excess heat through radiation. During cold weather the blacktail can reduce the blood flow and cut down on the amount of body heat that escapes through the ears' large surface area.

In the heat of the day, a jackrabbit keeps cool by dozing in a shallow depression called a "form," which it hollows out under a shady bush or cactus. At sunset it emerges cautiously and searches for food, stopping frequently to listen for predators. This goes on until dawn, when the jackrabbit returns to the shelter of a form.

The jack's multifarious diet includes grasses and succulents, the twigs, leaves, and bark of various trees and bushes, and such crops as wheat, corn, soybeans, and alfalfa.

Equally varied is the blacktail's list of enemies. They range from coyotes, bobcats, foxes, dogs, and the larger raptors, to farmers, hunters, and automobile drivers. Even snakes can catch young jacks, but an adult can usually elude crafty predators with its blinding speed. It can bolt through a thick mesquite field like lightning, zigzagging its way to safety at speeds up to forty miles per hour. Captain William Clark, on his expedition up the Missouri and Columbia rivers with Meriwether Lewis, measured the jackrabbit's leaps and found them commonly from eighteen to twenty-two feet.

Despite decades of persecution by man, a variety of natural predators, droughts, and epidemic diseases, the jackrabbit population is as strong today as ever. The transformation of prairie and desert to farmland has only provided it with a dependable food supply. Much like its natural enemy the coyote, the black-tailed jackrabbit probably will be able to continue to adapt to the agriculturization and urbanization of the West. Truly, the jackrabbit is no dumb bunny.

PIPING DOWN THE VALLEYS WILD

TEXT AND PHOTOGRAPHY BY DOUGLAS GRUENAU

The most social of the marmot species, the Olympic marmot packs a whole year's activity into four short months.

The opening phrase of William Blake's poem "Reeds of Innocence" suggests to me a spirit of mountains and valleys, a quality I feel when I hear the clear, sharp "whistle" of a marmot from its front porch in a steep mountain meadow. To a marmot this is an alerting signal, indicating there is an intruder in the area. It is not actually a whistle because the sound is made with the vocal cords.

Marmots are the largest members of the squirrel family and have the characteristic bushy tails. There are four to six species of marmots in North America, depending on which experts you refer to. The woodchuck is a marmot and the most solitary member of the group. The Olympic marmot, living only in the Olympic Mountains of Washington, is the most social species in the group.

Mountain marmots pack all of a year's activity into the summer. Emerging in mid-May from a true hibernation in which their body temperature and heart rate are significantly lowered, they begin to look for edible vegetation, hungry from their winter-long nap. An Olympic marmot colony usually has one adult male, several adult females, several yearlings, and a litter of infants. The area occupied by the colony contains several sets of burrows. One set of burrows is used as a nursery, and another set is used by the male and the other members of the colony.

These burrow complexes have several openings. The main entrance has a large dirt front porch on the downhill side, with a lush growth of sedges around it, probably stimulated by the earthworks. Off one of the tunnels is a sleeping chamber lined with sedges and other meadow plants. Scattered throughout the colony area are short, single-entrance burrows which can be used for a quick retreat from danger. Grassy trails connect the most frequently used entrances.

The colony's day begins when the morning sun has warmed the meadow. The adults emerge from their burrows and stretch in the sun on their front porches. They will often sit

"The mother often returns to the burrow, checking on the young. This leads to an extensive round of greetings initiated by the infants. They nuzzle the mother's nose and mouth, and she will part her lips, revealing yellow-orange teeth."

or stand up on their hind legs surveying the meadow, alert to possible danger. After the area has been checked out they gradually move to grazing areas, feeding in a loose group. Toward noon they return to their burrows, resting in the sun on their front porches before entering the burrow for the midday lull. They emerge again later in the afternoon to feed until sunset.

Frequently a marmot will pick a prominent rock on which to sun and rest. It is from these perches that we often hear a marmot whistle. When the sun is behind clouds, the marmot will hug the rock, which has been absorbing the sun's heat during the day, using it as a radiator.

The young first emerge above ground in late July. As if surprised at the visual feast they remain for only seconds at first, popping in and out of the burrow. Eventually they stay above ground as long as the adults.

In these first days the mother often returns to the nursery burrow, checking on the young. This leads to an extensive round of greetings initiated by the infants. They nuzzle the mother's nose and mouth, and she will part her lips, revealing yellow-orange teeth, the result of enamel deposits as she matures. The young marmots have white teeth. This greeting activity continues into adult life, though it is less frequent, and it probably helps maintain social bonds in the colony.

By late August all of the colony members are concentrating their energies on feeding, in order to store up enough body fat reserves for the winter hibernation. By late September or early October all colony members have entered one burrow to hibernate. By sleeping together they conserve vital body heat. Here they will remain for eight months, emerging in mid-May to begin another marmot summer.

"The colony's day begins when the morning sun has warmed the meadow. The adults emerge from their burrows and stretch in the sun on their front porches."

A CONTRARILY BRAINY BEAST

TEXT BY RUSSELL McKEE • PHOTOGRAPHY BY CARL R. SAMS II

"This is a difficult beast ... It has caused large groups of citizens to scorn other large groups who scowl and growl in return, despite few ever having howdied and shaken hands or listened to each other beforehand."

To maintain its reputation as North America's most controversial animal is not an easy assignment, but the white-tailed deer works at the task, and with sublime success. This animal has long been a magnet both for excessive praise and angry denunciation, for love at its mooniest and hate with its wildest eye. The whitetail is a delight to see afield, graceful in movement, a ballet artist on an outdoor stage. It is also a most contrarily brainy beast. It can make itself invisible anytime it wants, humbling more than eighty percent of the hunters who try to match its woodland wits. It seems able to survive any-where. Depending on plants available in nature's local supermarket, it will live a lifetime within half a mile of its birthplace; or it may range over miles and miles of real estate to gather its victuals.

The whitetail has caused the passage of more laws and regulations than one can count, and deer hunting is the subject of more heated arguments than any sport. The animal drives hunters to climb trees, sleep in snow, get lost, divorce wives, start fistfights. During hunting seasons, it produces brags and boasts and unsliced baloney from otherwise modest humans, and it occasionally turns a normally law-abiding person into an outright criminal. It has caused large groups of citizens to scorn other large groups who scowl and growl in return, despite few ever having howdied and shaken hands or listened to each other beforehand. Think about that: If you are not a deer hunter, do you hate all deer hunters on principle? And if you are a deer hunter, do you hate people who hate deer hunters? If yes to either of the above, blame it on the whitetail.

This is a difficult beast we are talking about here. Each autumn, American hunters do their best to quell the whitetail by shooting and dragging home two million of its kind. Each spring the whitetail responds by producing three million young to fill their place. It isn't quite like trying to empty Lake Superior with a garden hose, but pretty close. Most of the "surplus" above the hunting kill is lost to starvation, poachers, disease, and predation, but nonetheless total whitetail numbers appear to be increasing nationwide, year by year.

To about twelve million of us, the whitetail is *the* big-game animal of North America, the domestic safari-maker, the creature that produces racks that hang over fireplaces in countless homes. Deer hunting is a tradition, an industry, an economic bulge that hits the nation each fall. But to millions who are not inclined toward hunting, the whitetail epitomizes nature's joy and grace and beauty. It is an animal that always needs protection, especially against hunters.

Somewhere between those extremes lies an ever-changing political, moral, and biological battleground on which we struggle in dealing with this most fascinating and exciting animal. Meantime, despite all the controversy, there is one often overlooked point on which we all agree: Without the white-tailed deer in our midst, we would be a much poorer nation of wildlife enthusiasts.

In our midst the whitetail most certainly is. Deer, I'm sure you've noticed, are frequently seen in the suburbs these days, and they are especially numerous where tasty plantings of strawberries, turnips, carrots, apples, corn, and other desirables abound. Plant an apple tree and you plant a deer magnet. Plant an unfenced garden on the edge of town and you might as well assign half your crop to whitetails at the outset.

Commercial orchardists and truck farmers say a hearty amen to that. Sometimes they are allowed to make war on whitetails, wars which to my knowledge have never been won by humans. Bleary-eyed from nighttime chases, these agricultural agonizers give up after a time and set devices in orchard or turnip patch, timed to trigger firecrackers,

sirens, and bells. Then they go to bed. What happens? Whitetails jump and run when they first hear these alarms, then soon enough simply jump higher and grab more apples. In Wisconsin and several other states, hundreds of thousands of dollars have been paid in recent years to farmers for lost fruit and vegetables, but the payments seldom cover actual losses. Besides, that's not a good answer to the deer problem.

Such a remarkable animal is this white-tailed deer! Such a history, such a vital life-force! Its earliest forebears tiptoed out of the murk about 200 million years ago. Mammals developed from reptiles in that period, and being mammals ourselves we also carry a bit of that time in our own bloodstreams. But whereas our ancestors developed five toes for clinging and holding, the pigs and hippos four, sloths three, and horses only one, it was Cervidae, the deer, that grew two toes on each hoof, eight in all—a set of running shoes that provides them with great turning and maneuvering power as they dash and twist their way through trees and brush. The two toes per hoof also create those gracefully curving sets of prints left in sand, mud, and

28

snow—tracks sought by North American hunters from time beyond memory.

Today's sleek whitetail is far different from its forebears. Its earliest predecessor was a rabbit-sized creature that looked like a tiny greyhound and probably spent all its time eating or running from predators. As it changed form over thousands of centuries, it grew in size and began to lose a pair of long down-turned teeth exposed like tusks over the lower lip. As these tusks disappeared, a pair of knobby points developed on top of its skull. These points at first remained covered in furry skin and probably looked much like the knobs we see today on a giraffe's head. The giraffe, in fact, is a near-cousin of the deer. But in the deer, those skull points gradually grew longer, hardened, and became antlers. It was a curious physical change, and one that continues to puzzle zoologists. Rollin Baker, professor emeritus of zoology at Michigan State University, commented on it in the first chapter of the Wildlife Management Institute's *White-Tailed Deer: Ecology and Management,* published in 1984. "Strange indeed," wrote Baker, "was the course of evolution that developed the 'disposable' head adornments of the Cervidae, especially when 'permanent' ones, like the cow's horns, might have served the same functions. The antler growth process requires considerable expenditure of nutrients by the carrier. In fact, it seems almost too energy-expensive for the individuals to have endured, despite the fact that antlers grow, then as now, during the vegetative season, when foods are usually plentiful. Be that as it may, cervids have diversified successfully and persisted through four continents plus North Africa."

Zoologists now recognize thirty subspecies of whitetails in North America alone. They range in size from the tiny Key deer found only on islands off the southern tip of Florida to huge specimens found in several of our eastern and midwestern states. Mature Key deer average twenty-six inches tall at the shoulder and weigh sixty to eighty pounds on the hoof, about the size of an Irish setter. By contrast, in several states east of the Mississippi, adult whitetail bucks that weigh in excess of 300 pounds field dressed have been taken—which makes them 350 to 375 pounds on the hoof.

The whitetail has adapted to almost every type of habitat found in North America. Northeastern woodlands, coastal salt plains, mountain and farm country, tallgrass prairies and shortgrass plains, the Rockies from Canada to Central America—all are home to this deer. It is even beginning to overcome its long doubts about the Southwest, the West Coast, and the Great Basin lands of Utah, Nevada, and California. These are still the domain of the mule deer, but the whitetail continues to expand westward and occasionally may be seen anyplace there, except in the Central Valley and desert portions of southern California. Imagine, therefore, the variety of foods on which the whitetail is able to survive. For a long time, most observers classified deer as browsing animals, not grazers. As browsers, they were supposed to eat only twigs, leaves, and bark of trees and shrubs and leave all the grasses, sedges, and weeds to grazing animals such as sheep and cattle. But nowhere does the whitetail stick only to browsing foods. Plant remains found in the stomachs of white-tailed deer include just about every grass, sedge, forb, lichen, fungi, and moss known to the herbalist. The leaves and twigs of almost every tree, vine, and bush are its main courses, salads, or desserts. Even the berries of poison ivy and poison sumac are eaten—to say nothing of sourwood, chokecherries, soapberry, fleabane, greasewood, skunkwood sumac, and every other mean-sounding plant on the continent. But whitetails also consume all the sweeter-sounding plants as well: honeysuckle, sweet William, wild grape, American beautyberry, sweetbay, strawberry, blueberry, huckleberry, cherry, and rose.

How are these animals able to convert to flesh and bone such an awesome variety of plant life? The secret may lie in their habit of nibbling everything in sight but not a lot of any one plant. Follow a deer through the woods. It takes a bite of one plant, a bite of another, then has a bit of grass or a sniff and nibble of the nearest bush. Biologists believe that the stomach microorganisms of whitetails have evolved over the centuries so they are now able to digest just about anything. Thus when ax or plow or snow or flood or fire removes more common foods, deer can survive for lengthy periods on whatever remains.

Whitetails have not purchased this ability cheaply; only through starvation and disease has the deer we know today evolved into an animal so bountifully equipped for survival. Its production of young, given reasonable conditions, is phenomenal. Its variety of body size, range, and habitat—even the several colors, lengths, and densities of its body hair—all suggest a powerful ability to adapt. In eastern and midwestern woodlands, where food is plentiful, whitetails see little need to move about and so stay put, often for a lifetime. But on the Dakota flatlands, where lunch may be a long way from

"Hundreds of thousands of dollars have been paid in recent years to farmers for lost fruit and vegetables, but the payments seldom cover actual losses. Besides, that's not a good answer to the deer problem."

breakfast, young deer have been found to disperse to new range commonly twenty to thirty miles from their birthplace. One deer in Minnesota traveled 55 miles to find new range. In North Dakota another traveled 126 miles.

In our southern states, whitetail body hair is short; in the northern snowbelt it is long with added hollow guard hairs for extra insulation. In spring this heavy coat is shed. In shaded eastern woodlands, the deer's coat is darker, while on the open sunny plains hair color is light. This color variation serves the whitetail well when time comes for the deer's disappearing act. In northern woodlands deer blend in with the dark tree trunks; in cattle country, with the pale sage and mesquite; and on coastal plains, with tawny marsh grass and cattails. The only way to know if deer are present is simply to wait them out. That takes plenty of patience. But as every hunter and woods-walker knows, if you simply stand still long enough, eventually a deer will blow its cover.

The study of the behavior of whitetails, as distinct from biological research, is currently a field of intense interest. But it is also one of the most difficult to tackle. To understand behavior, students of the natural sciences must venture off the safe ground of objective study into a world tinged with human values. They must deal with concepts of deer "families" and "home" range and "social" activities—ideas that can't be measured in centimeters and degrees Celsius. Nevertheless, this is both a fascinating new arena and one to which many students of wildlife management have been driven by necessity. There have been thousands of biological studies over the last half-century investigating every conceivable internal fact of this animal. And there is growing criticism that far too much effort has been spent studying the whitetail's innards to the exclusion of more urgently needed wildlife research. On one recent count, nearly 350 individual whitetail studies were under way nationwide at a time when other wildlife research languished from lack of funds.

"It's the old question of who pays the lab technician," grumbled one frustrated wildlife student. "Deer hunters buy a lot of licenses and pay plenty of special equipment taxes, and a lot of that money filters back into test tubes, so there's always funds for whatever biological research on whitetails comes along. But if you want to study plovers or periwinkles, the money isn't there. This is a serious matter, because the piping plover, as one example, is threatened with extinction, yet there's almost no money avail-

able for basic research that might help save it." For many years, Michigan diverted some of its wildlife funds from deer to nongame species, until hunters began to grumble that they were being shortchanged. They were providing the money, and it was not returning to their sport. Now the state has a "check-off" box on its income tax form that allows citizens to allocate money directly to aid nongame species, and this has largely resolved the problem. Other states have similar programs. This is a different issue, of course, but it does show how the whitetail has become the dominant influence on American wildlife management.

As to behavioral research, some fascinating questions are cropping up. For example: Suppose research shows that the biggest, strongest buck is the center of an extended whitetail family that has one dominant buck plus a cluster of adult does, fawns, and yearlings. The dominant buck controls and impregnates most of the does, thereby spreading his strong genes through the entire future herd. This buck also keeps the so-called "family structure" intact by driving out the lesser, younger bucks, thereby broadening the geographic range of the herd. Most of this seems from field observations to be the case. But the dominant bucks are also the very animals most sought by hunters, and few of these trophy deer survive more than a couple of seasons. By removing such pivotal members of the whitetail family, this theory suggests, hunters may be causing internal herd disruptions sufficient to hold annual fawn production in check. Suppose further study showed that if we gave more protection to those dominant bucks, their does would in turn produce more large trophy deer, as well as larger summer herds through greater fawn production. By issuing only a limited number of permits for hunters to take "branched antler" bucks each fall, such protection could be accomplished, thereby forcing more hunting pressure onto the yearling and spikehorn deer.

This sounds plausible, but even if true, where might such fine tuning be used? Our application of the biological information we already have is pretty spotty. In many areas of the nation, bucks-only hunting is still desired by large numbers of hunters, reflecting an attitude that prevailed nationwide fifty years ago. And look at the patchwork history of our relations with this animal. In the year 1500 there were an estimated 35 million whitetails in North America. That number began to dwindle steadily as more and more immigrants came to settle here. The whitetail became the corner meat market on four legs. It was the primary food- and implement-producing animal of eastern North America. Meat, fat, bone, antler, hair, hide, and hoof—all were used for scores of purposes. The hair went into pillows; hide scraped thin covered cabin windows; antler was carved into toys, tools, and trinkets; and fat became candle tallow. It is fair to say that settlement of this continent virtually rode on the back of the white-tailed deer. In the West, it was buffalo that served these purposes, but the whitetail was of far greater importance to settlers. No pioneer family could have cleared ground, built a cabin, and produced that critical first crop had it not been for the white-tailed deer, always nearby to provide sustenance, clothing, and utensils.

As settlement intensified, however, whitetail use became overuse, and deer numbers fell sharply until about 1890. Then, only an estimated 300,000 whitetails remained nationwide, slightly less than one percent of the peak population four hundred years earlier. In fact, some observers believe that from 1850 to 1890 hunting exerted the greatest pressure ever put on a continent's wildlife. Both market-hunting and hunting for the pot were common year-round. Those were the years when the buffalo was decimated and the passenger pigeon was virtually eliminated. It was the period that gave new meaning to the word "gory," especially after Sir George Gore, an Englishman, arrived in the United States in 1854 with an arsenal of weapons and a retinue of "beaters." For three years he blasted his way through the great wild herds of what are now Wyoming, Colorado, and Montana. It could hardly be called hunting. Moving from place to place, Sir George would position himself in a blind in any likely looking location. Then his small army of beaters would drive local game toward him. Seated on a camp chair, Gore would fire at everything that approached. He would then hand the emptied weapon to a helper who would, like a surgeon's aide, hand back a loaded gun. Gore didn't even stop to eat; food was brought and he continued to fire between bites. History does not record how many thousands of buffalo, elk, deer, antelope, and other animals Gore downed during his rampage.

But that was the mood of the times, and for deer, market-hunting was probably the main destroyer. In the 1870s venison sold for only five to six cents per pound in Wisconsin and Minnesota. One report tells of a Minnesota father-and-son team who killed and sent to market six thousand deer in the year 1860. In addition, stewpot hunting of like mag-

nitude was widespread. Such market activity for whitetail meat, in fact, was the driving force that caused railroads to build refrigeration cars. So the whitetail had an important impact on railroads and meat marketing processes heavily used in later years during the cattle traffic from the West.

However, the days of uncontrolled hunting were coming to an end. In 1901 Teddy Roosevelt became President; together with Gifford Pinchot, John Muir, George Bird Grinnell, and a small band of like-minded men, he began the American conservation movement. The forests of America were

31

nearly gone, along with certain wild animals, so the public was aware of the problem, and conservation steadily took hold through the first thirty years of this century. We were still a nation of farmers and ranchers, so we understood plant and animal husbandry. As part of this understanding, the whitetail was given protection state by state. Until the mid-1930s, hunting of bucks was sharply limited. Does and fawns were given almost complete protection in most states. At the same time, the wildlands of America were recovering from the clear-cut logging of the 1800s, producing ideal brushy conditions over vast areas, the kind of habitat in which deer thrive.

The result was a spectacular production of deer. Never before or since has a major wild species increased so dramatically in such a short time. Food was plentiful, and female deer were protected. Counting deer became a popular springtime activity, with Boy Scout troops, service clubs, local citizens, and sportsmen's groups turning out to walk through local thickets, driving deer ahead to others who counted them. Such counts were regularly reported in local newspapers, though the counters' accuracy wasn't always the highest. However, at the George Reserve near Ann Arbor, Michigan, one well-documented study showed what was happening. The reserve is a fenced enclosure, not quite two square miles in size, composed of typical midwestern woodlands, marshes, and brushy, grassy openings. The soil was poor for agriculture but provided successful deer habitat. Two whitetail bucks and four does were released inside this area in 1928. In the next few years deer were seen occasionally, some with fawns, but managers hardly expected what they found five years later—an astonishing total of 220 bucks, does, and fawns.

The George Reserve was a capsule version of what was happening nationwide. Aldo Leopold's seminal book, *Game Management,* published in 1933, set down the principles of controlling deer herd growth. Those principles became gospel among wildlife managers and have been taught in universities across the land ever since. "Game management," wrote Leopold, "is the art of making land produce sustained annual crops of wild game for recreational use." Leopold proposed using the principles of crop production used in agriculture and forestry to produce maximum yields of game. Where possible, habitat would be adjusted to promote maximum yields. Hunting would be one of the implements used to "harvest" annual crops, so game populations could be held to the "carrying capacity" of the range.

Leopold's book grew out of concern over mounting public enthusiasm for doe protection. Leopold knew that the females had to be harvested along with the bucks. If they weren't, there would be a lot of range destruction, overpopulation, and herd starvation. But at that point a generation of Americans—and their children—had been taught a different gospel, protection. Now suddenly those same state game agencies that had taught doe and fawn protection were urging that the does and fawns be hunted. Didn't such agencies get their budgets from hunting license sales? Were they just trying to sell more licenses?

The controversy that followed lasted for another generation, and pockets of doubt and resistance are still found. Classic battles were fought, with hunters leading the fight against any-deer seasons. There were few "anti-hunters" in those days; it was the hunters themselves who lobbied legislators, who brought injunctions and carried placards. They were trying to restrict their own sport because they thought too much hunting, with doe seasons, would reduce the breeding population and destroy the herd. The fact that it was sportsmen, not preservationists, who fought to stop any-deer seasons is frequently overlooked in the current debate over hunting.

Through the 1940s, 1950s, and 1960s the battles raged, with state wildlife agencies being battered in the process. Some states used a special "camp deer" permit to help control growing herd numbers. It was issued to any four hunters who could then take an extra deer, usually a doe or fawn, for consumption in hunting camp. But still not enough does and fawns were culled from the herds. In 1952 Michigan tried yet another approach. During the last three days of the annual sixteen-day November deer season, any hunter who hadn't killed a buck could take a doe or fawn. In the public meeting at which this season was established, one of the conservation commissioners asked Harry Ruhl, chief of the Game Division, if the deer herd could withstand such a season. Ruhl paused, looked at his staff, looked at the audience of doubting hunters, and then in a classic statement summed up the situation: "Well, Commissioner," he said, "I'm sure the deer herd can stand it, but I'm not so sure the public can stand it."

He was right. Hunters took 96,000 deer in those three days, a time when cars still had fenders on which deer could be carried home. Nowadays, Michigan hunters routinely take 150,000 deer each year and nobody complains, but in those days the nor-

Shed antlers do not endure long in the wild, for they are storehouses of salts that are prized by mice, squirrels, and porcupines.

mal kill was only about 60,000. The sudden "mass slaughter" raised a storm of protest. In one month the Game Division received more than five thousand letters, some signed in blood, some containing threats of violence, some attached to brickbats. A rumor circulated that Ruhl had killed off all the deer in Wisconsin before coming to Michigan to do the same. He had never worked in Wisconsin, but that didn't slow the story. It was a classic case of government imposing scientific regulations on a public not prepared to accept them. Wildlife managers looked back, and sure enough, Leopold had said game management was an art, not a science. The politics of the hunting season had been ignored by the commissioners, and hard lessons were learned. Several years passed, in fact, before adequate harvests were authorized again, and in the interim the state lost hundreds of thousands of deer to starvation.

Nationwide we are now embarked on a corrected course of deer management that is working. But is the danger of oversell still present, as it was through two generations of protection of does and fawns? Dale R. McCullough, professor of wildlife at the University of California, voices one of his concerns: "As professionals, wildlife biologists and managers must distinguish between cases where hunting is necessary and where it is not. It is possible to recognize the legitimate interests and necessary roles of human hunters without becoming apologists or advocates for the recreation. Bias toward hunting in sit-

uations where hunting is not necessary can only result in loss of credibility. Professional integrity demands that no side of a controversy be given favor on biological grounds that cannot be justified by the biology of the case under review. If hunters are favored because they pay the costs of management through license fees and special taxes, let that be the justification, and not an indefensible position that hunting is necessary in cases where it is not."

Today, veteran hunters in some states still have doubts about the taking of does and fawns. Maybe in places they are right. And trophy bucks are still the great prize sought by most whitetail hunters. Maybe that's wrong. But the main thing to remember about the whitetail is the reproductive dynamo that whirls inside it. Despite heavy hunting and arguments against all hunting, despite drought, disease, predators, and starvation, despite court suits and television laments, nationwide the whitetail has serenely been expanding its range, filling niches, eating apples and turnips meant for you and me. We must be doing something right. We could call it sound conservation and pat ourselves on the back, but most of the kudos should go to the animal itself for being such a productive, if occasionally troublesome, member of our wild community. And whatever your personal view of hunting, that white flag you see each time a deer disappears into the brush is not a sign of retreat and surrender. Instead, it says, "Life's a joy, and I'm here to stay!"

TO EVERY THING
A SEASON

TEXT BY JOHN MADSON • PHOTOGRAPHY BY CARL R. SAMS II

A TIME FOR DOES AND FAWNS

The gestation period of the white-tailed doe is about two hundred days, and fawns conceived in November are born late in May or early June. When her time comes, the doe quietly leaves other deer and seeks solitude. If she's a one-and-a-half-year-old, she can usually expect a single fawn. An older doe in good condition usually bears twins, or even triplets. The entire birth is rapid and almost bloodless. From the time a fawn's head first emerges, only about three seconds may pass before it is fully born. The tiny fawn gains strength and awareness with astonishing speed. A two-hour-old fawn will begin nursing if the doe is lying down, and by the time it is a half-day old the fawn can easily nurse while the doe is standing. Deer milk is very rich, with about twice the solids of Jersey cow milk and nearly three times as much fat and protein. It is highly concentrated, but not much is available at one feeding, and so fawns suckle for short periods at frequent intervals.

When the fawn isn't feeding, its early life is a summer idyll that consists largely of resting, brushing away bugs, and waiting for the next meal. The doe stays with her fawn at night, but in the daytime she wanders off to eat and drink, returning often to nurse her young. A young fawn's bright bay coat, bro-

ken by about three hundred perfectly white spots, is almost total camouflage against the leafy, sun-dappled floor of a nursery thicket,

but the fawn's most effective defense is complete immobility and an apparent obedience to his mother's "commands" to lie quietly.

Fawns nurse heavily for nearly two months, but they may be completely weaned at three and one-half months.

May 23rd: The buds of an eight-point rack.

A TIME FOR BUCKS AND TINES

June 24th: Another month of growth.

Antlers are a buck's pride and glory. With them he is a lusty warrior. Without them he's a meek nonentity. Unlike the horns of sheep, goats, and cattle, a deer antler is solid bone that is shed and renewed each year. In the North, antlers begin to appear on the buck's brow in April and May, growing from a pedicel on the skull. The young antler is sheathed in a soft, velvety membrane that is highly charged with blood vessels that transport the building materials. An antler in "velvet" is tender, sensitive, and easily injured, and an injury will result in an indelible deformity.

As the antlers reach their maximum size in September, an increasing charge of the male hormone testosterone in the blood somehow ripens the antlers and halts their growth, causing the blood supply to be cut off and

July 22nd: Eight round points in tender velvet.

the "velvet" to dry and be torn away as the buck shadowboxes with trees and shrubs. The rack of a white-tailed buck shows a typical, symmetrical shape. Here, a heavy main beam arises from the brow, curves backward briefly, and then curves out and forward. The tines arise from this main beam. The final antler is solid, polished bone with some tines so sharp as to be painful to a heavy touch. While the buck carries such weapons he is domineering and dangerous. He is on the prod, swollen-necked and red-eyed, a splendid fighting machine.

October 17th: Eight sharp points of polished bone.

November: The No. 1 stag in pursuit of does.

In spring, summer, and early fall a deer herd ranges widely, roaming hardwood ridges and fattening on a hundred varieties of plant food. Shelter is of little concern; food is plentiful, and energy demands are easily met. But deer shrink from the raw, cold winds of early winter and leave the uplands to seek the protection of cedar swamps, dense stands of conifers, and the sun-bathed south slopes of ridges. Throughout the entire North, the greatest winter urge of whitetails is to escape

the cold. So they maroon themselves in deer yards. Only about ten percent of the total range may be used in winter—something like a human family deserting all other rooms in the house to huddle around the furnace.

In the thin sun of the short winter days the deer totter along the skein of trails in their yards. Their coats roughen, hipbones show, and great hollows appear in their flanks. Their eyes become dull, the jaws appear "mumpy," body fat reserves are gone, and the deer compete viciously for food. Bucks dominate does, does dominate fawns, even their own. If a fawn grows too weak to follow its mother through deep snow, the doe will promptly abandon it. The survival instinct is stronger than any maternal ties. And so the deer starve and die—two in this thicket, twenty in this deer yard, tens of thousands in a single state, and nearly two million nationally in a single severe winter. But cruel as winter may be, there is always spring.

BIRDS OF MANY FEATHERS

A TURTLEDOVE
IN A PINE TREE

TEXT BY LES LINE • PHOTOGRAPH BY GARY ZAHM

"It should not be surprising that a species so incredibly fecund is also subject to tremendous mortality. The hazards begin in the cradle."

In the spring of 1960, I launched my ornithological career. By shaking pine trees, yanking on boughs, kicking trunks.

As my mentor in matters of the feather had demonstrated, this was the tried and true way to find mourning dove nests. You had to rouse the brooding bird from its slapdash but well-hidden platform of twigs. My mentor was Gene Kenaga, entomologist, conservationist, and tireless bird-bander who seemed intent on tagging every mourning dove squab in central Michigan.

In that part of the country, mourning doves are mostly of one mind in their choice of nesting sites. Dense evergreens. Elsewhere, ground nests may be the vogue. A study of four Oklahoma counties located 64,760 pairs of mourning doves nesting on the ground and 26,730 pairs in trees. But in several years of dove-banding in Michigan, we came upon only one ground nest.

I was Kenaga's apprentice that spring, and together we banded 183 dove nestlings. Our evenings and weekends were spent driving from suburban backyards with their clustered spruces to pine-clad graveyards and Christmas tree plantations. From the standpoint of nesting success, the best sites are those close to human habitation. Oklahoma biologists found that young were fledged from only 15 percent of dove nests in wild areas, compared with a success rate of 50 percent in places like cemeteries and orchards. We found most nests within five to fifteen feet of the ground, but on occasion the nimble Kenaga had to ascend forty feet or higher to attach the aluminum ring that, for the rest of its life, would give a young dove an individual identity among the 500 million of its kind.

That life is likely to be short. Consider the history of mourning dove No. 673-40504, whose flimsy natal home was discovered six feet from the ground in a young red pine growing in my front yard.

In southern states, mourning doves nest year-round. But up North, there is a "key week" each spring when dove nesting takes off in a rush. What determines the key week is a period of several days during which the average low nighttime temperature rises from 37 degrees to 42 degrees. Nesting can occur earlier, but those birds are usually ones that wintered locally and are conditioned to colder weather.

The egg containing the cell of dove No. 673-40504 was laid in a cold drizzle on April 18, 1962. Fourteen days is the magic number for a baby mourning dove. Fourteen days in the egg. Fourteen more days before fledging. The female dove lays her first egg one afternoon, the second egg the following morning. A larger clutch is very rare; in a study of 736 Michigan dove nests, only three contained three eggs or young, and four infertile eggs were found in another nest.

It was a warm, sunny May 1st, with gaywings blooming in the litter of pine needles, when this particular egg was punctured from within and a newly hatched mourning dove struggled free of its shell prison. Both parents had shared incubation duties, the female staying on the nest at night, her mate relieving at dawn. And both would feed the squab. For the first day or two, the diet is pure pigeon milk—a nutritious white liquid, rich in calcium and vitamins, that is secreted from the lining of the adult's crop. Strangely, the male dove supplies more milk than the female; and among all the world's animals, doves and pigeons are the only species in which the male lactates to feed young.

But the doveling's diet is quickly supplemented by an increasing percentage of regurgitated seeds, insects, and worms. By May 14th, when dove No. 673-40504 left its nest, its diet was 95 percent solid food, and it had increased its weight thirty-fold.

For another week, the young bird was fed by its parents. But they already had begun a second brood in another pine tree a few yards away. In an average spring–summer season, a pair of northern doves will raise at least two and probably three broods. Moreover, a dove hatched early in the year is itself ready to breed by late summer. Having passed through a gradual molt of its juvenile feathers, the first-year dove is impossible to tell, on sight alone, from an adult.

It should not be surprising that a species so

incredibly fecund is also subject to tremendous mortality. The hazards begin in the cradle. Eggs and nestlings are destroyed by snakes, rats, skunks, foxes, cats, flying squirrels, crows, blue jays. Swarms of ants overrun ground nests. In a study of 680 mourning dove nests in Alabama, half were victimized by predators. Of those doves that fledge, many will perish in their first year. Natural predators, most notably Cooper's and sharp-shinned hawks, claim a fair share. Disease outbreaks and severe weather can take a toll of hundreds of thousands of birds; in 1951, when a winter storm raked the South, more than 63,000 dead doves were counted by 143 farmers in Tennessee alone.

And each fall, fifty million doves drop before the shotguns of hunters. The fate of dove No. 673-40504 was typical. On December 24, 1962—at an age of eight months, 800 miles from its birthplace—it was bagged near Snowdoun, Alabama, by a Montgomery physician, B. F. Dorrough.

In captivity, the bird that colonists called the turtledove, after a species so familiar to them back in England, can live a pampered life for fifteen years. In the wild, relatively few mourning doves survive three years. But another Michigan bird, banded as an adult on May 22, 1936, earned a footnote in the annals of ornithology. Each spring for the next five years it was recaptured in the same trap. That dove was at least six years old—an ancient and lucky bird indeed.

RAVENS
ON MY MIND

TEXT BY BERND HEINRICH • PAINTING BY ROBERT BATEMAN

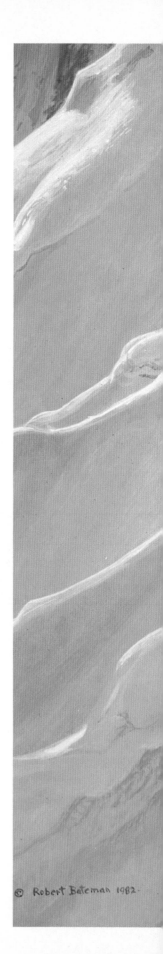

© Robert Bateman 1982

Snowflakes are lazily spiraling earthward, catching on the browned brittle heads of goldenrod, field spiraea, and fireweed. Only recently these plant skeletons had sported yellow, white, and purple flowers that stood out against the green grass. Bumblebees had scrambled over the flowers, frenziedly competing with each other for tiny droplets of nectar and pollen. This pollen and nectar had provided food to produce new queens, now underground, being gently covered by layers of cottony, insulating snow.

The woods are silent. The white-throated sparrow, ovenbird, and hermit thrush have flown south. Field and forest are left now for only the winter-hardy: chickadee, blue jay, coyote—and the northern raven, *Corvus corax.*

On this day, as on innumerable others this winter, my mind is on ravens as I peer across the snowy field through a crack between the logs of my unfinished cabin. A hundred yards in front of me, down by the edge of the woods, is their bait—two calf carcasses. Sitting for days on end in an unheated cabin, watching for a bird to come by and feed, is not very exciting—unless one is fired by a burning question. I am. Do ravens, possibly the most intelligent of all birds, cooperate with each other in finding food?

This question grew from a puzzling observation that contrasted with the foraging behavior of bumblebees, which I had observed in this field earlier. Like many other field observations it came as a pleasant surprise. I had been taking a casual walk on a cool crisp morning. Recently fallen leaves were tinged with frost, and my footsteps sank deep into them, making crunching sounds. I could hear blue jays calling from the ridge above. A flock of evening grosbeaks flew over to feed on beech trees whose trunks were scarred by the claw marks of black bears.

All was as I had remembered from countless other autumns in central Maine. Except now, in the distance, I heard ravens. But their calls were not just the usual *quork,*

quork, quork one hears from mated birds in their year-round territory. These calls were different. They sounded like high-pitched yells. There was palpable excitement in them, and they kept coming from the same place about a half-mile away. I did not need plainer language to understand that these ravens were calling about something that stirred them. Following their calls, I discovered it was a moose carcass, or the remains of one. A bear had torn into it, but the flesh was still fresh. The coyotes had not yet arrived. And in the meantime, more than twenty ravens were having a feast.

You can hardly miss a raven in these woods in winter, but I had not seen any for days. One bird could have found the carcass by chance perhaps. But twenty? My credulity did not stretch that far; I had to have a better answer. Even if twenty birds had found this carcass independently, that would not mean they would voluntarily share the feast, as anyone who has watched blue jays at a bird feeder knows.

The inordinately more abundant blue jays, a corvid relative of the raven, invariably fight for possession of or access to birdseed, or to any opened carcass. Yet it would make less sense for the blue jays—who do not rely on carrion during the winter as the ravens do—to fight over a carcass, because it is not vital to their survival as it is to the ravens'. Still, it is the blue jays that fight and the ravens that share.

Cooperation is common in the animal world, and it is often the key to survival in hostile environments. It is not difficult to envision how a strategy of cooperative foraging in ravens could be to their advantage. If twenty independently foraging ravens somehow communicated and shared each food bonanza they discovered, then any one raven would have a nearly twenty times greater chance of having food on a regular basis. In winter there is little else to feed upon except carcasses of other animals that have not survived. And since these carcasses

are rare, each one is cleaned up within several days by mammalian predators and scavengers. Thus, by sharing a kill the ravens are not giving up anything—because the greater part of any kill is a temporary resource that is consumed largely by others. To test the validity of this theory of cooperation I set out animal carcasses throughout the winter. A deer, a goat, or a calf would be consumed almost overnight after a pack of coyotes had found it, but one or a few ravens feeding hardly left a noticeable dent.

Superficially the woods near my camp in central Maine look no different now than they did twenty or thirty years ago. At that time, when I was an avid deer hunter, I already knew them well. On the light snow in November, the whitetail bucks wandered in search of does, and I trailed them through the beech-maple forests, down into the fir-cedar swamps, back up again through the hardwoods, and up onto the spruce-clad ridges. There were no tracks of major predators—no wolves, no coyotes, no cougars. And I never heard or saw a raven.

But things have changed in twenty years: The coyotes and the ravens have moved in, nearly simultaneously. From my camp I often hear coyotes howling at night. I see their tracks in the snow almost every day, and after about ten hours in the woods I often see a raven or at least hear one in the distance. Deer and moose are the common link for the survival of both coyote and raven in winter. But these animals were here before and were perhaps even more numerous than they are now.

There is much speculation about why coyotes arrived and settled here. The prevalent view is that they came from the northwest, interbreeding with wolves along the way and then filling a niche left when the wolves were wiped out. But why did the ravens come at about the same time? Was it because of some kind of association between the two?

I satisfied myself that no ravens would have been feeding on that moose carcass were it not for the predators that had ripped it open. Ravens have strong beaks, but they were unable to take more than the eyes and part of the tongue of an undamaged moose's head. Neither were they able to penetrate the hides of deer, goats, calves, or raccoons. Indeed, carcasses that were not ripped open by the ravens. Often a raven or two would come by for a brief daily visit, as if checking out whether or not feeding could begin. The ravens' association with some predators is well known. Ravens follow wolf packs, and they have been reported to be attracted even

to the howls wolves make after a kill. Eskimos claim ravens follow polar bears, apparently waiting for them to make kills. Because of the close relationship of ravens with predators it seemed conceivable that these birds could discover a dead animal, perhaps one that had died from starvation, and then make noise to call in a scavenger, maybe a coyote. The ravens rely on the predators to make a kill, or on scavengers to dig out animals that have died and become buried in deep snow. However, in my experiments all of the ravens that discovered whole carcasses remained silent. None tried to attract a scavenger. Clearly, the calling at the moose carcass was not meant to alert coyotes or bears.

Ravens have an immense repertoire of calls, and no lexicon of their sounds exists. However, one of their common family of calls at a rich food source, the "yelling," is similar to the "place-indicating call" described by the German scientist Eberhard Gwinner, who has studied captive ravens. He had observed the place-indicating call in fledgling young, who apparently use it to indicate their whereabouts to parents, and in the female at the nest. If the birds cooperate in food-finding, then it seems appropriate that they would also use this call, or yell, at a rich food bonanza.

There is no doubt that the calls can be a powerful attractant: I recorded the yelling the ravens made at an opened deer carcass and played it back in the absence of food. If ravens were nearby and not at other food, they usually came immediately, flying directly overhead. Clearly, if the ravens had wanted to minimize sharing the kill they could have merely kept silent. To be sure, there were occasional squabbles at a carcass where many ravens were congregated, but of greater significance than the squabbles was the fact that dozens of ravens routinely fed at a single carcass at the same time.

Cramped and cold, watching in my cabin since dawn, I find my scientific curiosity sorely tested. I long to see just one of the sleek shiny birds, to hear the swish of its wingbeats. It might be hours, or days, before one arrives. But one will arrive, sometime. It always does. After it does, how will it behave, and when will the others come?

This time I am lucky. Sometimes no raven appears for two days. But today one flies over at 9:40 A.M. It circles back and stays in the vicinity of the clearing for twenty-four minutes. Then it leaves. But three hours later it returns with a second raven, and the yelling commences. After an hour's silence, the ravens begin yelling again—more of them. By later afternoon I see four simultaneously.

None of the ravens descends to the bait. But then one makes a strange knocking noise that sounds like a metallic drum roll. The drumming continues at intervals of several minutes, and then I see a raven approach on foot out of the nearby woods. It gets almost up to one of the calves, then flies back nervously as if afraid, only to return in a few seconds for another approach. The bird is clearly frightened, yet hungry. A strange bait, like these calf carcasses, could easily hide a trap that has been set for coyotes. Do the ravens know of this danger from previous experience? Ultimately the raven retreats. None touch the calves this day.

The next day I resume my vigil. A raven is already calling in the nearby woods at dawn, and more can be heard yelling at intervals throughout the morning. Occasionally one swoops over the bait. More ravens come, after long intervals when none seemed to be in the vicinity. Near noon there are suddenly six of them. Four descend simultaneously, form a phalanx, and advance cautiously side by side on foot toward the closer carcass. With pointed beaks and outstretched necks, they continue to advance, until one pecks at the calf. Instantly they all jump up and take flight. But within fifteen seconds the four regroup for the same maneuver, only this time five others swoop in and join the original four.

It seems that all of the ravens want to feed, but none wants to be the first. Now the nine advance together on a broad front. Again the group takes flight after one of them pecks at the calf, and again they regroup for another advance. After several tries in short succession, they finally begin to feed, and by late afternoon at least twelve birds are coming and leaving independently.

The snow, which has been coming down sporadically, is now developing into a storm. By tomorrow morning the calves will be buried. Unless the birds can shovel snow, their feast will be brief.

Five inches accumulate during the night, but the ravens come shortly after dawn the next day. Six of them perch on the snow-covered branches of the spruces at the edge of the field. They sit in pairs, preen their fluffed feathers, and make soft croaking sounds. Others call from the nearby forest. The birds fly repeatedly over the site where the calves lie buried, and one lands there, jumping up and down nervously before leaving. By six o'clock they have all left. When no ravens can be seen I leave the cabin with my tape deck and loudspeaker, hide under some spruce branches, and play the raven "yelling" I had recorded earlier. In four out of six trials one or two ravens appear overhead within fifteen seconds. I have never seen a more beautiful sight than those ravens. Of course this has worked before already, but the implications are too important not to do it again, and again. To me it seems like a miracle each time.

The coyotes come the next night; I had heard them howl the previous evening from a neighboring ridge. Their story is written on the snow. They come as a group, and in two days there is nothing left of the calves. Where might the ravens feed next? In these woods that I have walked for many winters without finding more than one carcass, I do not envy them their task.

When I finally light the evening fire in my cabin stove I already feel warmed inside by the knowledge that the ravens' sharing behavior is indeed real, and that it is even more important than I had originally supposed. Their behavior results in an increase in the availability of food to each individual. It also serves to decrease the risk that any individual might face when feeding at an unfamiliar bait. Yet I still don't know the mechanism by which the sharing behavior evolved.

I think now of honeybees, which are more likely to land where others are already feeding, and which recruit at short range by broadcasting scent rather than sound. But how did the ravens recruit others from such long distances? Is there a raven "dance" that incites or invites followers at a communal roost? What were the drumlike calls? And what was their function? The raven, who cocks its head at me as it flies by along the ridge, now holds more secrets than ever before. And I have good reason to watch ravens for years to come.

"Cooperation is common in the animal world, and it is often the key to survival in hostile environments. It is not difficult to envision how a strategy of cooperative foraging in ravens could be to their advantage."

55

TOO MANY MALLARDS

TEXT BY ROBERT HOLLAND • PHOTOGRAPHY BY ROD PLANCK

Overpopulation always causes creatures trouble, especially when it is sustained by a dole.

It made sense at first—a few mallards to quack and paddle picturesquely around the three-acre surface of Mirror Lake; the Victorian solution to the chaos of an unfinished landscape, or at least something to add life to the University of Connecticut campus in Storrs. And when fall tailed into winter and the water began to slow and thicken into ice, those mallards, lured by feral relatives and shudders of instinct, would fly off to Chesapeake Bay. With any luck they would be back in the spring, vigorous and ready to set up housekeeping.

There was no reason to suspect it would work any other way. Oh, there was the chance they'd get turned into *canard à l'orange* on the way south, but there are a lot of ducks in the air then, and the odds seemed in favor of some making it back.

Those that did find a safe air lane through the barrage of number-four lead, steel, or copper-plated shot; that managed not to flatten themselves against the World Trade Center or collide with some misguided aircraft; that could find forage enough to fatten up for the return flight, would be assured of a safe haven on Mirror Lake. There they could raise their broods. People could come and marvel at the little puffballs and watch them mature into full-sized mallards. And what could it matter if people scattered cracked corn, bread, and doughnuts on the shore and in the water?

The trouble was that not enough people thought enough like ducks, and the people who did were not in control. No one considered what a reliable food supply might mean. Perhaps that is why it seemed so mysterious when, a couple of years later, the ducks simply gave up flying south.

It was a fall like any other, the season keeping to its schedule but for some minor hitches in and out of Indian Summer. Time scurried like dry leaves before the November wind, and as the sun settled into its low southerly arc the days grew shorter. A perfectly normal fall—except the ducks did not leave.

When the mornings were bright with frost and the still nights stretched an icy film over most of the pond, the ducks gathered at the inlet where the water escapes from its under-ground course, a good deal warmer for its passage. There they paddled back and forth, chatting among themselves until the first yellow shots of sunlight broke over the Fine Arts Building. Then they picked up, suddenly and irrevocably, in the way of all ducks, and flew up to Horsebarn Hill. The School of Agriculture had finished harvesting the corn there, and the ducks gobbled up the tidbits left behind. They supplemented that with excursions to a bank of red oaks across the road from the pond, where they found more acorns than they could eat. And they could always count on students for all sorts of strange handouts.

The first years the ducks stayed by the inlet throughout the winter. The flock was small, thirty or so, and the birds had room to swim around and chase and splash without compromising the individual distance each required. Ducks do not mind cold weather, and as long as they have food and open water they seem quite willing to avoid the hazards of flight. Probably that is because in nature a bird in the hand is always better than two in the bush. And that is the wrinkle which man has always used to exploit the rest of the animal world. Man alone can anticipate; he alone can understand when immediate gratification will lead to disaster. That explains why mousetraps work so well. Yet while man can certainly anticipate, he often does not take the trouble, and that explains why welfare works as well as mousetraps.

For the ducks it was a simple calculation. Keeping warm requires calories, and if they didn't have to expend much energy in finding food, they could use the calories to generate body heat. So began the great duck dole in Storrs. The ducks responded in the usual way, by making more ducks. Populations of animals tend to increase geometrically, parents producing offspring that become parents that produce offspring. As long as there is room and food this will go on unabated. The more ducks there were on Mirror Lake, the more people showed up to feed them.

In 1983, with the flock pushing two hundred, the ducks abandoned the inlet for a sheltered spot on the south side of the island where the water is only a foot or so deep. By late November the night ice began to hang

on through most of the day, growing steadily thicker until mere paddling could not keep the pond open. Duck droppings did that. Even the grim grip of January cold was no longer a threat. Unlike geese, which take care of these things on land, ducks leave their droppings in the water. As winter concentrated the contributors by freezing most of the pond, so it concentrated the contributions; the droppings ending up on the bottom to decompose and release heat. It was like having a giant, organic pool heater.

The flock grew...three hundred, four hundred, five hundred...and a local retired man began turning up with pails of cracked corn loaded in the back of his station wagon. Some thought he was right when he said, "If somebody doesn't feed the ducks, they'll starve during the winter. They don't know enough to fly south."

Implicit was the assumption that by making wild animals dependent you somehow override their genetic circuits and they forget what their harder-working relatives know. It doesn't work that way, of course, not for ducks any more than for humans. Stop feeding them, and eventually (usually following some internecine unpleasantness over available food) they'll begin moving on until population and food balance.

But because there seemed to be no upper limit on the food supply, the ducks on Mirror Lake saw no percentage in leaving. By the winter of 1985 the flock had grown to nearly eight hundred mallards, blacks, and hybrids, as well as about a dozen domestics. The result was a devastated pond, the bottom covered with several inches of feculent ooze that produced just the right conditions for great clouds of algae, which spent the warm-

er months billowing back and forth in the soft breezes tickling the surface of the pond. It was decidedly unpleasant to stand downwind of the water any time of year.

Curiously, the bird population also underwent some change. More than a hundred herring gulls stopped while migrating through—as gulls will do whenever there is a free lunch—and they were tough, voracious competitors. Last year three double-crested cormorants dropped in to wax fat on the goldfish stocked by departing students each spring. (Carp do well in pretty nasty water, especially if some salt is added now and again. The pond serves as a catch basin for several roads, so it gets a steady supply of salt during winter and when spring washes the roads with rain.)

The sight of other birds in large numbers and plenty of sprouting rye grass on the fields also drew in some Canada geese ...twelve hundred at one count. Add to that the local pigeons and crows, grackles and starlings, and instead of a placid campus pond ringed by lush green lawn, dotted with sweeping willows and sugar maples and white ash, the place resembled a soup kitchen for the extremely hungry but not-yet starving. They had plenty of spunk, and the bickering was harsh when the food arrived.

That should not have been surprising. Overpopulation always causes creatures trouble, and when it is sustained by a dole— when what began as unanticipated bounty becomes a right—behavior deteriorates quickly. The gulls and the geese and the cormorants, the grackles and starlings, moved on as winter drew the string of cold and ice ever tighter. But the ducks did not go.

Perhaps if someone from biology could ex-

"The trouble was that not enough people thought enough like ducks, and the people who did were not in control. No one considered what a reliable food supply might mean."

"There was only one way to solve the problem. Cut off the food supply, forcing the ducks to follow the instincts they had been encouraged to ignore."

plain birth control to these birds they would willingly limit the size of their families. But no one seems to speak Duck, which, after all, is a very difficult language. Not that they would listen anyway. No, there was only one way to solve the problem. Cut off the food supply, forcing the ducks to follow the instincts they had been encouraged to ignore.

Then Mirror Lake might take its place as a safe breeding area, propping up the flagging duck population at a time when drought and the destruction of wetlands to create more farmland have helped bring it to a thirty-year low. Wetland destruction is a very thorny problem. Competition for food is always a competition for space, and that applies whether the animals are foragers or growers. In this country there are people who think such a concept does not apply to humans. In China, some feel, only the suicidal would not apply the concept to humans. Perhaps if someone from biology could explain to humans in this country the need for birth control, people would willingly limit the size of their families. No one seems to know the language. Perhaps there is no language. But if,

in this matter, nature were called upon to arbitrate, everyone would soon understand the price. For when nature calls its creatures to account it has but a single goal, balance. In securing that balance it often enough extracts unconditional surrender.

The solution for the ducks on Mirror Lake was not nearly so dire. The university asked people not to feed the ducks and negotiated an arrangement with the man who fed them corn. It rounded up all the domestic ducks and those wild ducks that could not fly and housed them until homes could be found. This took twenty-four hours. In a month the population fell to four hundred. To eat they had to disperse. In this quiet corner of northeastern Connecticut there are more than a hundred dairy farms. And because hurricane Gloria flattened so many cornfields, allowing only a partial harvest, there was abundant food. It was also an especially good year for acorns.

But what if... what if there were no place to go that did not already have too many ducks? The answer is simple enough. That is when nature collects its due.

CORN AND QUACKERS

PHOTOGRAPH BY GARY ZAHM

You say your crop was too big for your bins? You had to pile corn out in the open where it might spoil? Cheer up, neighbor. Your problem is being handled by Mallards, Inc., specialists in short-term corn storage. They're right on top of the situation. Each worker can store up to 40 kernels of corn in a weatherproof compartment. Shipment by air freight, no extra charge.

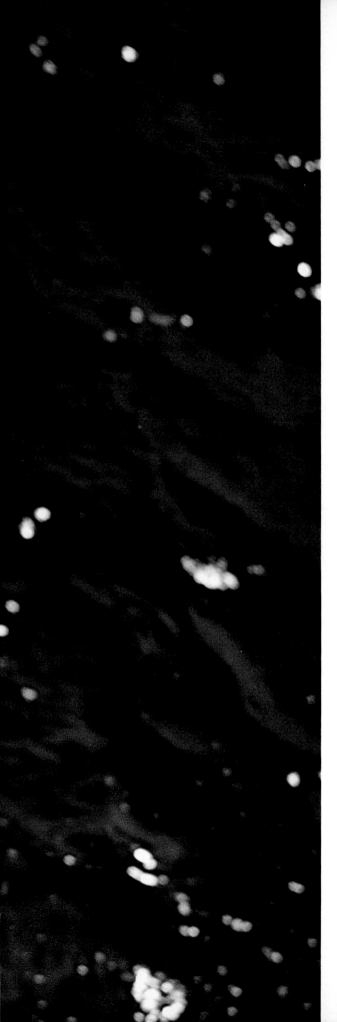

LONGTAIL

TEXT BY LES LINE • PHOTOGRAPHY BY TUI De ROY

Bosun-birds, sailors called them, and there are two explanations for that name. One is that their long central tail feathers suggested a marline-spike—a pointed iron tool used by the boatswain for separating strands when splicing rope. The other is that their shrill calls imitated the whistled signals from the boatswain's pipe. Wrote Robert Cushman Murphy in *Oceanic Birds of South America:*

"After weeks off soundings, in tropical blue waters where birds are scarce, the voyager may sometimes be electrified by hearing the shrill whistle of the Boatswain-bird. Looking aloft, he may see one, or perhaps a pair, of the gleaming, long-tailed creatures passing high in air on steadily and rapidly beating wings. On such occasions, according to my own experience, the visitors are likely to show a certain brief curiosity in the ship, and will turn off their course in order to fly in an oval orbit around it once or twice before streaking away like animate comets."

"Longtail is the Bermudian name for these black-and-white birds," William Beebe wrote in his classic book *Nonsuch: Land of Water.* "One of the most useless characters I can imagine is the long, attenuated central pair of tail feathers. It surely can be of no courtship value, for these birds court and mate in midair, almost always two males in fierce rivalry. Under these circumstances it is difficult to imagine any nice adjustment as to admired length, resiliency, or sweep of the feathery ornaments. The plumes are exceedingly tough and rubbery, as they must be to resist the wear and tear of constant attrition against the narrow ledges and rocky tunnels."

Bosun-birds or longtails, Murphy and Beebe both were describing tropicbirds, atypical members of the order Pelecaniformes. Indeed, some ornithologists question their close kinship to pelicans, cormorants, anhingas, boobies, and frigatebirds.

"One of the most useless characters I can imagine is the long, attenuated central pair of tail feathers... The plumes are exceedingly tough and rubbery, as they must be to resist the wear and tear of constant attrition against the narrow ledges and rocky tunnels."

—*William Beebe*

63

Said Murphy: "They differ much in habitus from all their existing relatives, and share many superficial characters with the terns. These include form and size, the shape of the beak, the silky sheen of the plumage, the voice, and aerial grace. Furthermore, tropicbirds hatch from the egg covered with down, instead of being naked like young boobies, cormorants, and pelicans."

There are three species: the white-tailed (or yellow-billed) tropicbird, which Beebe knew at Bermuda; the red-tailed tropicbird; and the red-billed tropicbird, here photographed by Tui De Roy on its nesting islands in her Galápagos homeland. The genus, Murphy wrote, is "well-named after Phaethon, the son of Apollo, who hurtled from the far sky into the sea. I remember the July day long ago when . . . I first saw one of a pair of red-billed tropicbirds dive from the height of the *Daisy*'s masthead into the quiet, transparent water. For several seconds it remained below and, after reappearing, shook a shower of pearls from its feathers, rested at the surface with wings spread and raised, and tail plumes cocked up, and finally leaped into the air as lightly as a tern."

The red-billed tropicbird is the largest of the trio, and whether they are useless as Beebe suggested, the feathers that stream eighteen to twenty inches behind the pigeon-size body are objects of wonder and beauty. Moreover, the streamers may indeed serve some function in display flights, when two birds will leave a high-circling group and glide toward the sea, the upper bird with its wings (and perhaps its streamers) bent down, the lower bird with its wings arched up until only two or three inches separate the wingtips of the pair.

Contrary to William Beebe's observation of over a half-century ago, mating does not occur while the birds are in flight. Beebe did, however, leave us a lyrical description of how the plumage of a tropicbird seems "to change color as rapidly as the squid upon which they feed, for when they fly over our white-washed laboratory roof their breasts are as immaculate as snow; over the shallows their plumage takes on the faintest, most delicate of pale chrysoprase, and far out from land, where the water draws its color from a full mile depth of ocean, reflection touches the plumage with a bubble-thin tint of ultramarine. When we see a tropicbird in full plumage on its nest in sunlight, a new color impinges upon our retina—we can no longer call its breast and tail white, and we cannot say that they are salmon or pink—the delicacy of this new real tone survives no humanmade name, it is sheer beauty."

Red-billed tropicbirds typically nest in cliffside niches that may be several hundred feet above the sea. (On Ascension Island, they nest in short burrows dug through accumulated layers of guano; and on Christmas Island, white-tailed tropicbirds raise their young in tree cavities.) A single egg is laid. And though they may be tough and rubbery, the streamers, Murphy records, "become broken or badly worn from the cramped quarters of the nest-chamber, and the fact that the quills of the females obviously fare worse than those of their mates may indicate that females habitually undertake the larger share of the labor of incubation."

Like the breeding plumes of egrets and herons, the tropicbird's streamers once attracted the attention of hunters for the millinery trade. And island natives treasured the tail feathers, wearing them in their hair or sticking them through a hole in the nose.

Tropicbirds are unable to walk or stand upright. They launch themselves by dropping from a ledge, like that shown with resting bird on page 49. To reach the jumping-off place, Murphy writes, "they push along on their bellies, spreading their wings as props and balancers."

During its two months in the nest, the tropicbird chick is fed regurgitated squid and fish. Parent birds leave for their feeding grounds before sunrise; some will return to the nests by mid-morning, but other birds foraging fifty miles or more from their home islands may not be back before dusk. When the young fledge, tropicbirds wander hundreds of miles from land, leading a wholly pelagic life until the next breeding season.

Far at sea they may circle with curiosity over a research ship, but their presence is likely to go unnoticed, most certainly unheralded. Few contemporary scientists, engaged in coldly analytical chores, would react to such an encounter with the joy of a Robert Cushman Murphy or William Beebe. For their writings we must be grateful.

III
INSECTS AND SUCH

EGG-LAYING THE HARD WAY

TEXT BY ALEXANDER B. KLOTS

·

PHOTOGRAPH BY CHARLES KREBS

A female long-tailed ichneumon wasp (*Megarhyssa lunator*) pushes her three-inch-long ovipositor deep into a maple trunk. In the wood are tunneling larvae of the pigeon tremex (*Tremex columba*), a large horntail sawfly—the "host" (really the prey) of the ichneumon.

People have long been fascinated, and a bit puzzled, by the ability of these wasps to locate the burrows of sawflies and lay their eggs in them. Contrary to previous beliefs, the ovipositor is not driven through solid wood but instead is merely slipped along cracks or into holes bored by the sawfly when it laid its eggs. Still, the highly complicated ovipositor mechanism must probe very skillfully and with much force. From the ichneumon egg hatches a grub that fastens to a sawfly larva and lives on it, eventually causing its death. (In turn it may be parasitized by tiny ibaliine cynipid wasps.)

Megarhyssa lunator is common in much of eastern North America; other species in the West parasitize wood-boring sawflies in conifers, and the group is distributed worldwide. One European relative was introduced into New Zealand to control destructive horntail sawflies. Large *Megarhyssa* females may have bodies one and a half inches long with their ovipositors more than three and a half inches. They are our longest wasps, but not our bulkiest. The ovipositor, incidentally, cannot be used as a stinging weapon. Occasionally the wasp is unable to withdraw her ovipositor and dies at her post of duty.

CHILDREN OF THE SUN

TEXT BY EDWIN WAY TEALE

·

PHOTOGRAPHY BY FRANK COCCO JR.

After more than a hundred million years on Earth the dragonfly asks no more of life today than it did in the age of the dinosaurs. Sunshine and living insects are the twin needs of its existence. In a world of infinite change its wants have remained the same.

The transformation from the underwater nymph to the aerial dragonfly is almost as amazing as though a trout should suddenly shed its skin and become a robin. Usually this miracle occurs during the heat of the day, although a few dragonflies emerge at night. In either case they climb from the water and cling to the bank, a stick, or weed while the suit of chitin armor splits down the back and the wings, damp and crumpled, unfold. Then, when the glistening coat has hardened, the insect darts into the sunshine. It leaves behind the ghost of its other self.

The shining wings, on which the dragonfly rides, are supported by a vast network of veins. In a single wing there may be as many as 3,000 separate cells between the veins. The insect skims through the air with one goal in sight, appeasing an insatiable appetite for living food.

The dragonfly is still a creature from the distant past. It rushes through the air, scooping up its victims in a basket formed of spine-fringed legs, sucking their bodies dry and

Facing page: green darner (Anax junius); *right: Sympetrum dragonfly and grey treefrog, both products of a recently completed metamorphosis.*

Facing page: amberwing (Perithemis tenera); *above: a wet-meadow dragonfly of the genus* Sympetrum.

letting the carcasses fall to the ground, all without slackening its headlong pace. Its great compound organs of sight may contain as many lenses as the eyes of 15,000 men. Its head, resembling half of a hollowed-out marble, is attached to the slender body by a sort of ball-and-socket joint that enables the dragonfly to turn its head almost completely around and see below as well as above.

The larger the dragonfly, the higher it hunts in the air. The smaller species skim so low above the water that trout and other game fish sometimes leap into the air and catch them on the wing. Bullfrogs also snap them up when they come too close, and the webs of spiders snare the smaller dragonflies. The larger ones, however, break through and escape. In the words of an old Japanese poem: "Through even the spider's fence, it has force to burst its way."

In northern states the first cold of fall kills off these children of the sun. Only the nymphs remain in their underwater home to carry on the chain of life. Lingering old age is virtually unknown in the world of insects. There is no wasting decrepitude, no long deterioration of powers. For the dragonfly there is only the swoop of an enemy or the numbing anesthetic of autumn cold.

—*From "Grassroot Jungles," 1937*

Above left: black-faced skimmer (Libellula cyanea)*; left: widow* (Libellula luctuosa)*; right: brown-spotted yellow-wings* (Celithemis eponina) *on timothy.*

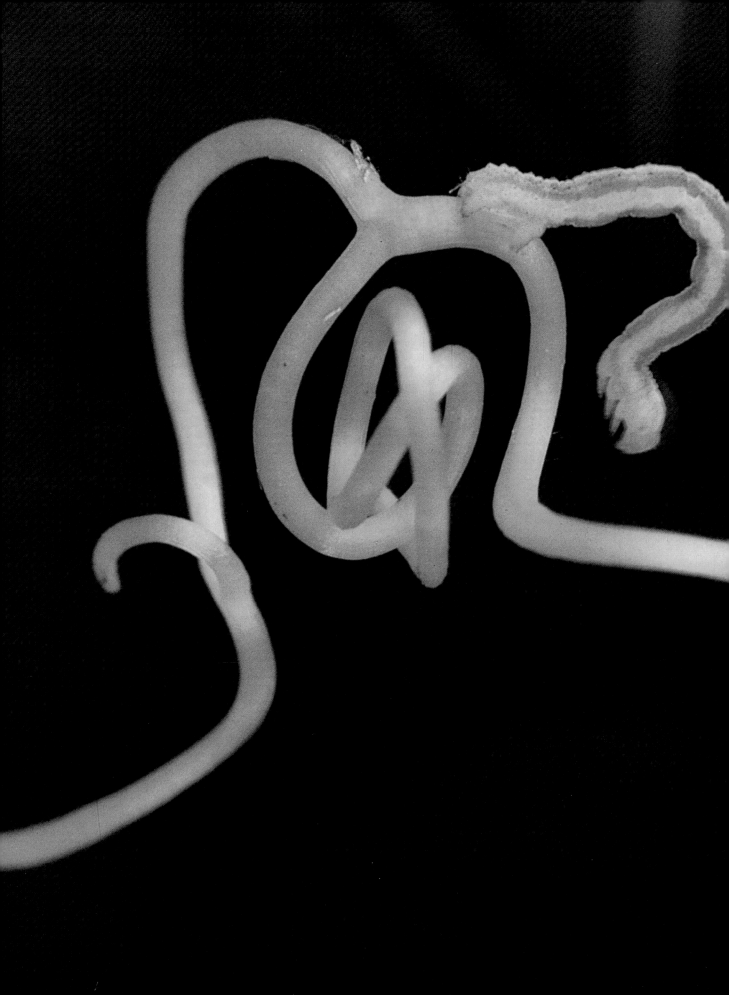

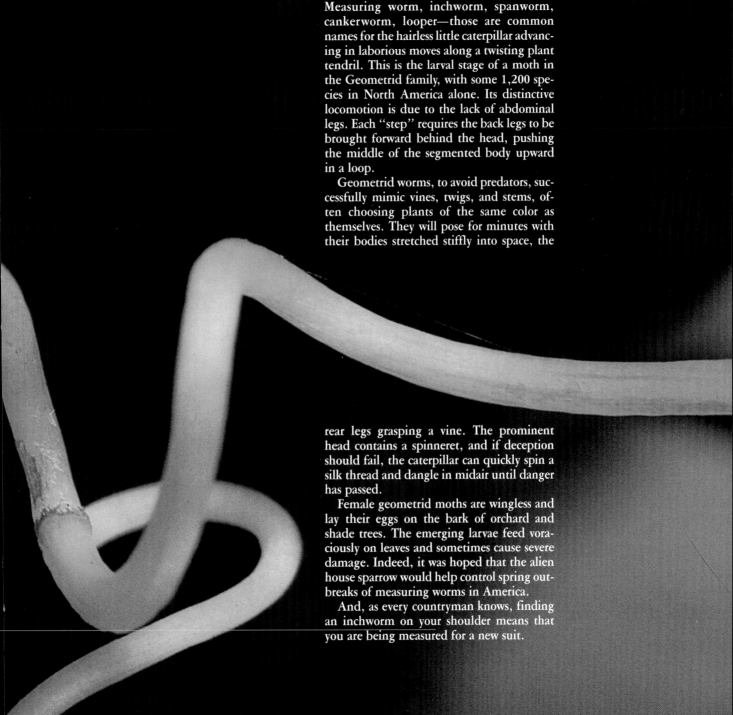

Measuring worm, inchworm, spanworm, cankerworm, looper—those are common names for the hairless little caterpillar advancing in laborious moves along a twisting plant tendril. This is the larval stage of a moth in the Geometrid family, with some 1,200 species in North America alone. Its distinctive locomotion is due to the lack of abdominal legs. Each "step" requires the back legs to be brought forward behind the head, pushing the middle of the segmented body upward in a loop.

Geometrid worms, to avoid predators, successfully mimic vines, twigs, and stems, often choosing plants of the same color as themselves. They will pose for minutes with their bodies stretched stiffly into space, the

rear legs grasping a vine. The prominent head contains a spinneret, and if deception should fail, the caterpillar can quickly spin a silk thread and dangle in midair until danger has passed.

Female geometrid moths are wingless and lay their eggs on the bark of orchard and shade trees. The emerging larvae feed voraciously on leaves and sometimes cause severe damage. Indeed, it was hoped that the alien house sparrow would help control spring outbreaks of measuring worms in America.

And, as every countryman knows, finding an inchworm on your shoulder means that you are being measured for a new suit.

IV

LIFE IN THE WATER

SUMMER OF
THE POLLYWOGS

TEXT BY T. H. WATKINS • PHOTOGRAPHY BY ZIG LESZCZYNSKI

Mating wood frogs (Rana sylvatica)*, the female heavy with eggs. The eggs in the foreground were laid by other pairs.*

I live these days in Washington, D.C., in a neighborhood that is so extraordinarily bucolic it is difficult to believe that this neighborhood exists in the heart of one of the nation's major cities. Just outside the door of our walkthrough brownstone flat is a tiny park-like area, an untended pocket wilderness of trees and ferns and bushes, so green in the spring and summer that it can hurt the eyes. At the backside of the apartment is a screened porch that looks out on an enormous pair of white oaks, complete with a population of birds and squirrels whose antics give our two pussycats room for bright-eyed speculation.

The street outside our front door is tunneled over with trees—acacias, maples, and chestnuts—and my two-mile walk to work each morning is through a celebration of chlorophyll. All of this means something

special to me. I came here after six years of living in New York City, amid its immutable concrete, its deforested streets, its lunatic subways, its crowds upon crowds upon crowds, people rubbing against people like erasers obliterating a lesson that did not need to be written. I feel somewhat rehumanized now, energized by oxygen and laughter.

So I walk down the tree-laden streets, an escapee, full of myself and open to possibilities. Such as the frog.

I saw him under a bush on my way to work one morning. He had crawled out from beneath a nest of leaves quite as dull-green as he was. He sat there on the edge of the sidewalk for a long time. He looked at me, not blinking. I looked at him, blinking. He was seduced by frog thoughts and had a destination in mind. After about twenty seconds, he hopped across the street and disappeared into a neighbor's garden. I wished him good flies—even while thirty-five years slipped away from me like snakeskin.

The frog's eyes were a time machine, something out of Ray Bradbury, a tunnel at the end of which a light still burned. You keep forgetting how much you remember, particularly from the childhood years. But it is all still there, like rising dough in the mind. So, the frog.

I was father to frogs once. This curious happenstance came about during my eleventh year, in Colton, California. This was a dry country, high-desert country, and one not much given to frogs. But there was a collection of ponds about a mile from my house, ponds fed by mineral springs, green with algae and life—and pollywogs. A friend had told me that frogs come from pollywogs. This was, of course, ridiculous. How could such inkblot creatures with their tiny tails ever become anything as complicated as a frog?

Still, I had to find out. In truth, I had been trying to find out about such things for much of my embryonic life. Small things especially. Ants, for example. They enchanted me, quite as much as if they had been tiny human beings with too many legs. There were three varieties available in the vacant lots which I haunted in the four or five square miles of Colton not surrounded by groves of orange trees: brown ants, red ants, and black ants. These were not their official Linnaean classifications, of course, but you have to admit that my terminology had a grace of simplicity not found in the notable Latinate work of the Great Classifier. You had your brown ants, your red ants, and your black ants.

Brown ants were minuscule things, distinguished mainly by their periodic invasions of our kitchen in extraordinary army files to carry off everything edible in sight and drive my mother to the pump-handled poison spray-gun (this was the pre-aerosol age). Red ants—and they really were a splendid bright magenta color—were my favorites. They were larger, with perfectly visible mandibles and the ability to give you one hell of a sting. They had *presence,* those ants. Every now and then I would filch a Mason jar out of my

A broken-striped newt feasts on wood-frog eggs. These explosive breeders lay their eggs in a frenzy and then vanish from the pond.

Wood-frog eggs five days old—and twenty-four hours before hatching. The voice of the wood frog suggests a quacking duck.

mother's kitchen and with a trowel desecrate a red-ant nest, filling the jar with a mixture of ants and dirt. I had not the wit then to understand that if I did not get hold of the queen ant in such an excavation, the worker ants I did manage to trap would not live long, nor would my miniature colony. But they always lasted a time sufficient to give me days of fascination, as their instinctual mechanisms put them into a frenzy of tunneling and nest construction until death.

And they had a smell, those hard-working, glass-imprisoned ants. I could take the lid off the jar and sniff it: an acrid, tannic smell strange to the nose, unlike anything I'd known before or have known since. I learned later that it was formic acid, one of the ingredients in the hard shells of their abdomens, thoraxes, and heads—the very essence of their construction. All I knew then was that ants had a smell, a wondrous thing.

Curiosity is the cruelty of children, and I might as well get this next out of the way. I was not only the warden of ants, I was their general. I, who now am the pacifist of the universe, I, who now wear anti-nuke T-shirts to my local pub, was as a child a warmonger. True. I would on occasion scoop up a colony of red ants and haul them off to a black-ant nest and dump them on the top of it. The resulting Stendhalian battle was a marvelous thing to witness. Both species were fierce fighters, and by that I mean to the death. But the black ants always won. They were larger and had mandibles half again as capacious as those of their opponents. What is more, they were protecting their own territory, and warriors are always more lethal under such circumstances. *Allons, enfants de la Patrie, le jour de gloire est arrivé . . .* In any case, after half an hour or so, the field would be littered with the dismembered bodies of

red ants. It is astounding how long a red ant can walk around without a head.

Ants. Curiosity. Cruelty. Now, back to the pollywogs.

One morning in this early summer of my eleventh year, I stole yet another of my mother's Mason jars, together with a small kitchen sieve, and marched off to the mineral-spring ponds a mile from my home. A diminutive Frank Buck after the elusive pollywog. I got him. I got hundreds of him, a school of inkblots swimming around in the greenish water of my Mason jar. God knows how many were crowded into the glass. Walking home, I realized I might have a problem on my hands.

I had read in one of the volumes of my *Book of Knowledge* set about the infestation of mice that once afflicted the south of France in the 19th Century. During one year, the population of mice in the region had blossomed to such an extent that the animals could no longer live with one another. They went crazy. They scattered out into the countryside, throwing themselves in front of cats in suicide attempts. After a while, the cats became so sated with mouse-meat they ignored the desperate little creatures, possibly burping, which is not a normal feline trait. The overbred mice died out nevertheless.

I contemplated my jarful of critters. It would not do to have in my possession a bunch of maddened pollywogs. What to do with them in order to watch whether they could develop into the fat fly-eaters my friend had said they would become? The solution was at hand. A few months before, my father had done some remodeling around the house. Our bathroom was part of this project, and along the way the old claw-foot bathtub had been ripped out, to be hauled off to the public dump sooner or

Newly hatched wood-frog tadpoles, showing their tufted gills. Wood frogs are found in wet woodlands and tundra ponds.

Wood-frog tadpole at three weeks, when the transformation to the adult stage begins.

later. My father had not yet gotten around to disposing of the great chunk of porcelain, and it reposed in a far corner of our backyard beneath a wizened peach tree which had not in memory been known to bring forth fruit.

I stuffed the drain-hole of the pocked and battered old tub with rags, filled it with water from the garden hose, then dumped my wriggling pollywogs into it. They burst and swam in the freedom of new space. Thereafter, once or twice a week I went back to the ponds from which they had sprung—rapidly becoming puddles as summer wore on in this arid climate—and hauled back a jarful of the green water, shrewdly guessing that pollywogs had to eat *something,* and that what they ate was doubtless in the scummy environment in which I had found them.

I was right. They thrived. And they changed before my very eyes, but not at first in the direction I had been led to expect. No, they became fish, turning a color closer to brown than black, developing visible gills. I was thrilled. Obviously, I was raising a tubful of the bluegill and crappie that my father and I would occasionally go out to catch at four o'clock in the morning from the various lakes that dotted the San Bernardino Mountains. We'd be sleepy and cold then, and I, delighted to be doing this man's work. What a gift I could now bring him!

I became obsessed with my crop of pollywog-fish. At break of day I would leap out of bed and crawl into my T-shirt and blue jeans. Then I would run out to check up on them. Such early risings and expeditions were not unusual with me in those days. For that spring, I had planted a row of morning glories along a stretch of our backyard fence not far from the decrepit bathtub. I loved to get up in the morning in time to watch the sun touch their blossoms into life and see the vines which held them creep and quiver upward against the fence. Those vines grew as I watched, cell being piled upon cell like stones in a country chimney. I would often sit and observe this heart-stopping thing until my mother called me in for breakfast.

No more. My incipient fish took all my attention. But then something terrible happened. The fish took on legs. They were not much, at first, just stubs. Yet the beginning of legs, there was no getting around it. Then eyes. I had expected eyes, but these were no eyes that had appeared on any fish I had ever known personally—little black bulging beads on the foreheads of my pollywogs. What was going on here?

Frogs were what was going on here. My friend had been right, the little wretch. The stubs soon became legs with tiny webbed feet attached. The eyes soon protruded above rounded frog-snouts. The pollywog tails soon eroded away, leaving nothing but standard frog-bottoms. I was left with a bathtub full of inch-long adolescent frogs.

Just what I was going to do with them was a question that came to mind. There may

have been a hundred of them now frolicking in the tub. I was riven with uncertainty. I could hardly stuff them into another Mason jar and carry them back to the mineral-water ponds, most of which were by this end of the summer cracked-mud memories. I needn't have worried. The frogs began to leave on their own. The strongest ones first. I noticed one morning that there were not quite as many still teeming about in the tub. Then one afternoon I was shocked at seeing an extraordinary exodus, one so compelling that it seemed to have been arrived at by common consent.

They left, the miniature frogs, they just plain left, all of them, crawling up the sides of the tub and jumping out over the rim, then scattering about in all directions. Although I tried to catch them, the task was impossible. They were too many, too fast in their tiny hopping. Within an hour or so they were gone. God only knows how many survived, how many escaped the predation of frog-eating birds or neighborhood cats, how many made it back to where they had been pollywogs unmolested by curious eleven-year-olds. To this day, I am convinced that it was there they wanted to be. I think I cried. I was only eleven years old, and it may have occurred to me then that I had been tampering with something larger than anything I had any right to touch.

When the Washington, D.C., frog disappeared into the neighbor's shrubbery, I turned my steps back toward the clatter and bustle of the city where my office lay, my mind pregnant with memory. I wish I could report that—when as a child I watched my pollywogs become fish, then stubby-legged swimmers, then tiny escaping frogs—I felt some Darwinian insight into the antiquity of life, some hint of the fact that we had been many things before we became what we are, some ancestral memory of the fish that learned to walk and became us. I felt none of these things, of course. Any validity such thoughts have comes purely from hindsight.

But I do think I learned something important the summer I midwifed inkblots into frogdom. The experience gave me at an early age the sense that all of us poor creatures on this Earth are interdependent, vulnerable to the pressures we can inflict on one another. I think I learned that we mess around with the natural order of things at our peril, and at the peril of the life that surrounds us. I think.

Well, maybe so. There is one thing I can tell you for certain: There was a question that nibbled at my mind as I walked the street that morning down to the grumble of traffic that is Pennsylvania Avenue, and it is a question with me still. Will I ever know so much of life again?

The wood frog at five weeks, now with a "robber's mask," occurs from Alaska to Labrador, and south into the Rocky Mountains, Ozarks, and southern Appalachians.

85

A SALMON DELIGHTS IN GAUDY COLORS

TEXT BY TOM ROSENBAUER • PHOTOGRAPHY BY G. ALLAN BROWN

Above: the Silver Wilkinson; facing page: the Jock Scott.

One hundred years ago, a large female salmon hung suspended in the current of a river in the south of England. She had been born in that river, worked her way downstream to the ocean as a tiny parr three years before, and had traveled thousands of miles before returning. She had not eaten in a month, since she entered the river. The complex of chemicals in the river, as distinct as a fingerprint, had led her to this pool, her birthplace, by her olfactory sense.

A parr, the same size she had been three years ago, flickered in front of her. She moved to it with barely a shiver of her sleek body, opened her mouth, and crushed the parr. There was no malice or hunger, it was a reflex, honed by tens of thousands of years of survival. The parr was killed not because it was important to her now, but because it would be a month later, when she would be laying eggs in the gravel bed and parr would cross back and forth, eating the genes of her future generation.

Another parr swung in front of her. This one did not look quite like the first but her reflexes did not discriminate. As she pounced there was a sudden pull on her jaw, and she burst through the water in fright, turning upside down before she crashed to the surface. If her sense of smell were as tuned to feathers as to the ions of her home river, she would have been able to detect bustard from southern Africa, three species of pheasants from China, fruitcrow and cotinga from the jungles of Latin America, turkey from North America, and grey jungle-fowl from India. All of them, parts of the same feathered lure that stuck in her jaw.

As you walk into the American Museum of Fly Fishing in Manchester, Vermont, your eyes are drawn to reds and greens and blues so brilliant they rival butterflies or tropical birds. There are hundreds of Victorian salmon flies mounted in shadow boxes and protected by glass, part of the Joseph D. Bates Jr. collection on loan to the museum. Unlike most flies used for fishing, which are drab counterfeits of obscure aquatic insects of interest to no one except trout fishermen and entomologists, these colorful attractors are painstaking replicas of feathered lures that were in vogue with English and Irish salmon fishermen at the turn of the century. Classic Atlantic salmon flies are enjoying a revival that is more than merely nostalgic, for they are the most ornate and pleasing artificial flies ever created.

The evocation of butterflies as well as tropical birds is apt. George Kelson, called the high priest of the Victorian salmon fly, postulated that salmon, which do not feed when they ascend freshwater rivers from the sea to spawn, would strike butterflies, moths, and caterpillars that fell into the water. In *The Salmon Fly* (1895), Kelson listed patterns for 250 different salmon flies. Most consist of many exotic bird feathers. To tie a Baron, for example, a fly-dresser would need to obtain the following feathers: ostrich herl, "Indian crow" (fruitcrow), blue jay, two types of feathers from a golden pheasant, swan, mandarin duck, peacock wing, mallard, "blue chatterer" (cotinga), neck feathers from an Indian junglefowl, blue macaw wing feathers, and claret-dyed hackles from a domestic chicken. Then he'd have to get some thread, silk floss, and silver tinsel, but these items must have been easy to find once he had the feathers in hand.

A friend became interested in these flies a couple of years ago. He was a fearless ironworker, walking girders hundreds of feet above the ground, until a bridge collapsed on an interstate highway, killing two of his best friends and leaving Pete hanging from a girder for several minutes. He couldn't go back to work and, as part of some self-prescribed therapy, began tying the most intricate flies he could find. Knowing I also had an interest in salmon flies, he talked me into taking a special course in tying the Victorian patterns from Bill Hunter of New Boston, New Hampshire. I had caught two Atlantic salmon in my life. Pete had never even gone salmon fishing and said he didn't intend to—he just liked the flies.

While ten of us sat around two card tables for a day and a half, spellbound, I realized that not all of the construction of the Victorian salmon fly was frivolous. The golden pheasant crest, curving over the top of the fly, holds every other feather in place vertically and frames the fly in a translucent halo. The macaw wing fibers, placed along the sides of the fly, hold the fly's wing fibers in place laterally. The underwing of turkey or pheasant tippets is carefully placed, used as a brace for the small slips of colorful goose or swan feathers. Even the order in which the tiny slips of bustard, swan, teal, and wood duck are put together is important, as some will not adhere properly, or "marry," to others.

But we didn't have swan or bustard or macaw. We used hen hackles dyed to match the natural colors of Indian crow and toucan and blue chatterer. For bustard we substituted the secondary wing quills of a wild turkey, and for English jay we used guinea hen hackles dyed blue. Some of the feathers Victorians used are available today, so we completed our patterns with genuine wood duck, teal, golden pheasant, Lady Amherst's pheasant, and ostrich—all domestically raised or legally hunted.

Why we could use some feathers according to the original patterns and had to substitute for others is a story that is tied up in the history of the American conservation movement and in the current laws of interstate and international commerce.

How did the luring of a salmon to a feathered hook reach such excess? Salmon had been caught on artificial flies since the 15th Century or earlier, but the flies were simple concoctions using drab feathers like snipe, partridge, and bittern. By 1658 Richard Franck, a soldier in Cromwell's army, observed that the salmon "delights in the most gaudy and Orient colors you can choose." In his memoirs Franck described the flies he used for salmon and recommended feathers from chickens, partridge, peacock, pheasant, mallard, teal, snipe, parrot, heron, parakeet, bittern, flamingo, and macaw. Where Franck got his materials is not known, but he must have been very well traveled or have befriended a sympathetic sea captain.

By the middle of the last century, salmon flies could be divided into two types: somber flies for times when the fish were supposedly feeding on aquatic insects, and bright, gaudy flies for inactive periods when the salmon needed to be aroused into striking. (Despite empirical evidence to the contrary, suggested by the fact that salmon were always caught with empty stomachs, salmon fishermen a century ago still believed that salmon fed constantly on their spawning runs.) Much to the disgust of traditionally minded anglers, flies with wings of mixed feathers, usually of contrasting colors, began to come out of Ireland. The "Irish fly" was even banned on Britain's River Tweed, because those who held the fishing rights on the river considered these flies "a kind of bugbear to the fish, scaring them from their accustomed haunts and resting spots." But the gaudy flies won out, at least until the end of the Victorian era.

Soon, fly-dressers were competing with one another to create the most extravagant patterns. It was a status symbol to a Victorian angler to have a killing pattern that his peers could not own because their fly-dressers could not obtain a bird-of-paradise skin at short notice. Eventually, it became easier to obtain exotic feathers as the millinery trade began buying feathers from around the world at a rate that would never again be equaled. British ships returning from around the empire would be greeted by eager fly-dressers, looking for a new and colorful feather.

The competition for special patterns increased as salmon fishing became fashionable. Kelson caught the spirit of the period when he stated that "there is no vocation that claims for its contingent a finer race of men than Angling—level-headed Britons whose lives are superior to those of lower fortune more by the graceful exercise of generous qualities than for their immediate possessions; it is quite certain that no sport has gained favour with fashionable folk so fast as Salmon fishing."

Fishing was elevated from a rough sport to a pastime of royalty. Men descended on the rivers wearing bowler hats, bow ties, three-button tweed suits, and either breeks (breeches) for fishing from the bank or wading stockings of waterproofed canvas with heavy brogues. The Princess of Wales and her daughters set the fashion for the ladies. *The Daily Telegraph* described their outfits:

Gowns made with skirts to the ankle, loosely fitting coats and blouses, are the kind of garments which these Royal ladies usually wear for fishing . . . The coat is of tweed, with lapels and cuffs of porpoise hide, and it is bound with this leather-like substance and furnished with many pockets; for the ardent Fisherwoman likes to have everything she may require at hand . . . The luncheon must be easily portable, and is usually confided to the attendant, but most women, knowing the strain that such continued exertion imposes, carry nourishment in a compressed form, furnishing their pouches or satchels with frame-

Facing page: Green Highlander on a grey junglefowl cape.

89

TREASURES FROM A FLY-TIER'S ATTIC

1. Great argus pheasant, Asia
2. Denham's (speckled) bustard, Africa
3. Vulturine guineafowl, Africa
4. Red-tailed (magnificent) cockatoo, Australia
5. Andean cock-of-the-rock, South America
6. Denham's bustard
7. Denham's bustard
8. Great bustard (florican), Eurasia
9. Toucan, Central America
10. Lovely cotinga (blue chatterer), Central America
11. Ocellated turkey, Central America
12. Red-ruffed fruitcrow (Indian crow), South America
13. Grey junglefowl (jungle cock), India
14. Satyr tragopan, Himalayas

A modern version of the Laxa Blue salmon fly was tied with (clockwise, from lower left) blue-dyed gray squirrel, silver tinsel, fluorescent-red rayon floss, blue rayon floss, golden pheasant tippets, and blue-dyed chicken hackle.

food tablets, or meat lozenges, or such things as they most approve for the purpose, besides a small flask of sherry or claret in their possession, as it would be awkward to want food or drink on one side of the stream with the attendant carrying it on the other.

But the Victorian salmon fly never became an important part of the American sporting life. Until after the Civil War, field sports were lumped with cock fighting, boxing, and horse racing as idle pursuits of the lazy or foolish. Fishing and hunting were still part of the frontier ethic, practiced for subsistence or commercial sale.

The coming of the industrial revolution gave the emerging middle class more leisure time, and fishing with the fly became an accepted if not desirable pastime. But the American fly-fisherman had to be satisfied with trout and bass, because most of the salmon rivers of New England had already been destroyed. Salmon lost their habitat to dams and to the scouring ravages of logging drives. In *Fishing With the Fly*, by Charles F. Orvis and A. Nelson Cheney, published in 1883, came this comment on just how dear salmon fishing was, even a hundred years ago: "Wealthy Americans in private yachts steam away to the tributaries of the St. Lawrence...the humbler citizen, with more limited purse, betakes his solitary way to the rehabilitated streams of Maine."

By the 1890s there were many trout flies of American origin, simple constructions of two or three brightly colored feathers. Mary Orvis Marbury, who wrote the definitive book cataloging American fly patterns, tied a collection of flies to be shown at the World's

91

Columbian Exposition at Chicago in 1893. The original flies are in the collection at the American Museum of Fly Fishing, saved from the ravages of moths and dermestid beetles by an airtight framing job. Commonly used were feathers from gamebirds such as turkey, mallard, teal, and goose; barnyard birds, including peafowl, chicken, and guineafowl; and songbirds such as blue jay. A few patterns were tied with more exotic feathers like those of the ibis, golden pheasant, and grey junglefowl—not the sort of feathers an Irish fly-dresser might covet.

Apparently the few Americans who were fortunate enough to afford salmon fishing had to order their salmon flies from the other side of the Atlantic. Mary Orvis Marbury, who was in the fly-tying business and quite adept at self-promotion, must have felt that the salmon-fly market was not large enough to warrant the acquisition of all those fancy feathers. For the rivers of Maine and Canada, she recommended all English patterns and suggested that anglers "order them from Mr. Forest of Kelso, Scotland."

Some American tiers were trying to develop the salmon fly in America, notably the expatriate Englishman J. Harrington Keene, who gave a complete list of feathers necessary for tying Victorian salmon flies in an 1887 edition of the American sporting magazine *The American Field.* But the most unusual source in Keene's list was not an exotic from a faraway jungle but an owl: "The eyebrows of this bird form a very beautiful species of hackle for the legs of many of the medium-sized flies that I make."

Where did the fly-tiers of the last century get their feathers? Poring over early fishing tackle catalogs, I can find no lists of fly-tying materials until the William Mills catalog of 1921. The 19th Century catalogs like those of Orvis, Thomas Chubb, Abbey and Imbrie, and Allcock listed rods, reels, leaders, and finished flies, but no materials for making flies.

I asked Paul Schullery, an angling historian who is writing a definitive history of fly-fishing, where the 19th Century fly-tiers got their feathers. He admitted we really don't

know much about where they got their materials, but suggested that a hundred years ago, when there was no refrigeration and we had a large rural population that hunted, everyone was in more frequent contact with animals. Many of the birds that we consider songbirds appeared regularly in markets and butcher shops. He also suggested that most of the 19th Century fly-tiers who were producing flies in any volume had contacts with the taxidermy and millinery trades. Both concerns advertised in the sporting periodicals, stating that they had fly-tying materials available but listing no specific kinds. "Send requests," was how they most often solicited orders.

There was no shortage in numbers or kinds of feathers. On one day in 1886, the ornithologist Frank Chapman counted 542 out of 700 women's hats decorated with feathers or even corpses of one or more of forty species of birds. An article in *Science* that year stated the writer had seen thirteen female passengers in a Madison Avenue horsecar with hats that included the heads and wings of three European starlings; an entire bird, spe-

cies unknown, of foreign origin; seven warblers, representing four species; a large tern; the heads and wings of three shorelarks; the wings of seven grassfinches; one-half of a gallinule; a small tern; a turtledove; a vireo; a yellow-breasted chat; and ostrich plumes.

Several things assured that salmon flies with fancy feathers would never become widely used in America. One happened in Washington, D.C., and changed the meaning of the word conservation forever. Another occurred on the salmon rivers of Atlantic Canada, and the third took place in Iceland. These last two would have no consequences for anyone but a salmon fisherman.

In the last part of the 19th Century, the noose began to tighten around the feather trade. Ironically, the same sportsmen who were buying and tying flies helped to dry up their own sources of supply. To understand what took place it is necessary to realize that fly-tiers don't create markets. They are scavengers of whatever feathers and furs are cheap and widely available. Fly-tiers un-

This oil still life of Atlantic salmon flies and tying materials, painted in 1890 by Englishwoman Catherine M. Wood, is on display at the American Museum of Fly Fishing in Manchester, Vermont.

A fly-tying box and an 1874 fishing license that belonged to an Irish sea captain.

doubtedly contributed to the demand for ibis, heron, and crane feathers, but their demand was a pittance compared with that of the millinery trade.

George Bird Grinnell, editor of *Forest and Stream* magazine, took one of the first initiatives to protect nongame species of birds and wildlife with the formation of the first Audubon Society in 1886. In a front-page editorial, his first sentence stated that "very slowly the public are awakening to see that the fashion of wearing the feathers and skins of birds is abominable." He documented the case of a single taxidermist who collected 11,018 bird skins in three months. By 1888 the society had some fifty thousand members, many of them sportsmen. The Audubon Society was so successful that Grinnell had to discontinue it in order to continue his editorial duties. But individual states, led by Massachusetts, formed their own organizations. In 1905 many of the states banded together, forming the National Association of Audubon Societies, the original name of the National Audubon Society. Grinnell became a director.

As early as the 1870s, individual states had passed laws to regulate the enormous slaughter of birds for plumage. Until the turn of the century, however, there were no laws that regulated interstate commerce in wildlife. The Lacey Act, a milestone in American conservation, was passed in 1900 after four years' debate. Authored by Representative John Lacey of Iowa and Senator George Hoar of Massachusetts, it sought protection for all species of songbirds by prohibiting the interstate transportation of "birds, feathers, or parts of birds to be used or sold."

While the Lacey Act regulated interstate commerce in feathers, it wasn't until later in the first quarter of the 20th Century that the taking of birds for their plumage was prohibited. The Migratory Bird Treaty, concluded with Great Britain in 1916, gave the federal government authority to regulate the taking of all migratory birds. It established a closed season on migratory gamebirds between March 10th and September 1st, and gave complete protection to all species of songbirds. The treaty took effect on July 3, 1918.

Local guides in Atlantic Canada, who knew little about fancy feathers and expensive tackle, were, for pragmatic reasons, making all this fuss about feathers moot from a fisherman's point of view. As politicians and sportsmen in the states were fighting to eliminate the feather trade, Canadian guides were making crude, simple flies from whatever materials were available.

These "fox-smelling lures" or "guide patterns," as the wealthy sports disdainfully called them, were made from strands of wool from old sweaters or blankets, with wings of hair, notably of hair from black bear, skunk, squirrel, and fox. The sports who were adventurous enough to try the new patterns instead of their British flies were amazed to find that the hair patterns frequently outfished the gaudy feathered lures. The use of hair in salmon flies was not new, as Richard Franck had recommended "dogs and bears heir" in his dressings nearly three hundred years before. But apparently Victorian fishermen, blinded by tradition, had largely ignored hair as a tying material.

Even in England, Victorian excess was giving way to a more pragmatic, Edwardian style. An Englishman named Ernest Crosfield, who fished the salmon rivers of Iceland, favored a salmon fly that exhibited no ornamentation that didn't also have fishing value. His flies, surprisingly similar to those being created across the Atlantic, were also sparse and simple, but held to the tradition of feathers rather than hair. His patterns featured a single internal wing of dyed goose or swan, sheathed with a speckled feather from a mallard, teal, or pintail.

Crosfield-type patterns and Canadian hairwing flies dominate the fly boxes of modern salmon anglers. But most fishermen still have a couple of Green Highlanders or Jock Scotts tucked away in a corner of a box, to share with friends and to preen and admire the beautiful feathers. There are more good tiers of classic Victorian patterns today than there were ten years ago. Despite the unavailability of most of the exotic feathers, they make do with a combination of dyed substitutes and the duck and pheasant feathers that are legal to buy and sell.

What determines the supply of feathers today? It is a complicated, often confusing system that "requires a Philadelphia lawyer to understand," according to one retailer of fly-tying materials. Rather than trying to look up all the laws involved, most people who sell fly-tying materials rely upon the U.S. Fish and Wildlife Service. John Harder, head of the fly department at the Orvis Company in Manchester, Vermont, one of the largest fly-tying retailers in the country, has found the people in the Fish and Wildlife Service more than willing to help if he has a question about the legality of a particular feather. Jim Sheridan, the special-agent-in-charge at Fish and Wildlife's Boston office, told me, "We seldom have any problems with fly-tiers or people selling fly-tying materials. Most of the time it's a guy who has bought a single

pheasant skin in England. They're legal here and in England, but unless the buyer has a permit to import the pheasant skin under the quota system established by the Tariff Classification Act, we have to seize the skin at customs."

And misunderstandings do occur. Dick Surrette, a fly-shop owner in New Hampshire, traded fishing tackle for woodcock wings from birds that one of his customers had shot during hunting season. He hung them up next to his mallard, grouse, and wood duck wings—which are perfectly legal to buy and sell. A man came into his shop twice, looked around, but never bought anything or talked to anyone. On the third trip, he walked over to the counter, paid for two pairs of woodcock wings, pulled out a badge, and declared that he was from the U. S. Fish and Wildlife Service. Surrette was in violation of the Migratory Bird Treaty Act.

How could Surrette legally sell wood duck and not woodcock? The original wording of the Migratory Bird Treaty Act said that it was "illegal to offer for sale the part of any migratory bird." But, tucked away in subpart J, 20.91, under "commercial use of feathers," it allows the sale of "migratory waterfowl for the making of fishing flies and similar commercial uses." Woodcock are migratory but are not waterfowl. They fall between the cracks, and even though they are legally hunted gamebirds, their feathers cannot be sold.

The grey junglefowl, or jungle cock as fly-tiers call it, is another interesting case. The Tariff Classification Act of 1962 made it illegal to import the feathers of any wild bird, with exceptions made for a quota of 45,000 skins of six species of pheasants, 1,000 skins of mandarin duck, and 5,000 skins of grey junglefowl per year. The junglefowl grows an unusual waxy hackle that looks as if it were painted with several coats of shiny lacquer. Jungle cock was de rigueur in most Victorian salmon flies.

In 1967 the Indian government became concerned about the harvest of grey junglefowl, which was taken for food as well as for its feathers. Export of any part of a grey junglefowl was prohibited. Two years later, the U.S. and British governments announced import bans on grey junglefowl feathers, and American enforcement agencies clamped down swiftly and effectively. With the passage of the Convention on International Trade in Endangered Species in the mid-1970s, India's export ban became an import ban in every nation that had signed CITES.

Three years ago, an enterprising Englishman named Ron Taylor, an amateur or-

nithologist and fly-tier, obtained some grey junglefowl eggs and began raising junglefowl commercially. After many problems with fertility and diet, he began selling capes in England for up to eighty dollars each. He arranged to sell his capes in the United States through a small mail-order company in Washington State. The company even took out ads in fishing magazines proclaiming "legal jungle cock." Apparently no one had checked with the Department of Commerce. Even though the feathers were domestically raised and legal in England, under the Tariff Classification Act the quota remained at zero and the capes were still illegal to import. Fly-tiers will have to wait until a fancy bird breeder finds out how to raise these birds in our climate.

As feathers become harder to obtain, the salmon fly will get simpler. One of the most effective new salmon-fly patterns is made by lashing blue- or yellow-dyed hair from the tail of a white-tailed deer to a clear plastic tube obtained from a disposable ball-point pen.

With the exception of several species of pheasants and the feathers of legally hunted birds like teal and wood duck, it is illegal to buy, sell, or import the exotic feathers used in the Victorian salmon fly. But it is not illegal to *possess* any feather except those from bald or golden eagles. The exotic feathers still turn up—passed on from a grandfather to a favorite grandson who ties flies, or in the attic of some widow who sells an old fly-tying chest in a tag sale—enough of them to keep the craft alive. Some tiers may be working from skins of birds that were killed when George Bird Grinnell was still alive. Salmon fly-tiers have also been known to court the veterinarians who clip the wings of the tropical birds in the aviaria of large metropolitan zoos.

These feathered lures are too breathtaking to be lost to history—even if the salmon don't care.

Lady Amherst

V

NATURAL PHENOMENA

CURTAINS OF LIGHT, HORSEMEN OF NIGHT

TEXT BY WALTER SULLIVAN • PHOTOGRAPHY BY MICHIO HOSHINO

Space shuttle astronauts photographed the aurora australis—southern lights—in May 1985.

But, where, O Nature, is thy law?
From the midnight lands comes up
  the dawn!
Is it not the sun setting his throne?
Is it not the icy seas that are flashing fire?
Lo, a cold flame has covered us!
Lo, in the nighttime day has come upon
  the Earth.

What makes a clear ray tremble in the night?
What strikes a slender flame into the
  firmament?
Like lightning without storm clouds,
Climbs to the heights from the Earth?
How can it be that frozen steam
Should midst winter bring forth fire?

With these words Russia's great 18th Century poet–scientist, Mikhail V. Lomonosov, described the aurora borealis, or northern lights, whose extraordinary displays even he, though far ahead of his time in understanding electrical phenomena, was unable to explain. "Who but God can conceive such infinite scenes of glory," wrote the 19th Century polar explorer Charles F. Hall. "Who but God could execute them, painting the heavens in such gorgeous display?"

Few natural phenomena are as awesome in scale and grandly beautiful as the ever-changing curtains of light that hang in the sky during an auroral display. For those living in the auroral zone at high latitude, as in Fairbanks, Alaska, Fort Churchill on Hudson Bay, and northern Scandinavia, visible auro-

ras are common, particularly during the long winter nights and when a major eruption on the sun has disrupted the magnetic field of the Earth. It is easy to understand why many northern peoples believed the multicolored displays were sunlight reflected off the polar ice. The Norse regarded the dancing lights as Valkyrie riding across the sky. According to Eskimo legends they represent wild ball games being played in the heavens by departed ancestors.

After a solar eruption the aurora can spread far enough south to be seen in Cuba and the Mediterranean. The Second Book of the Maccabees describes what is thought to have been a prolonged aurora over Jerusalem. According to that account, in the Biblical Apocrypha, for almost forty days "there were seen horsemen running in the air, in cloth of gold, and armed with lances, like a band of soldiers, and troops of horsemen in array, encountering and running one against another with shaking of shields, and multitudes of spikes, and drawing of swords, and casting of darts, and glittering of golden ornaments, and harness of all sorts. Whereupon every man prayed that the apparition might turn to good."

Magnificent auroral displays were familiar, almost 2,000 years ago, to the Roman writer Seneca. "These fires," he wrote, "present the most varied colors: Some are white; others scintillate; others finally are of an even yellow and emit neither rays nor projections." They sometimes resemble flames beyond the horizon which, he said, "is what happened under the reign of Tiberius, when the cohorts hurried to the succor of the colony of Ostia, believing it to be on fire."

Today, thanks to recent discoveries from space and on the Earth, we realize that the auroras are not supernatural but are to a large extent generated by the sun, 93 million miles away. It has been known for some time that the aurora's rays, glows, and rippling curtains of light are produced by extremely high-energy particles (electrons and protons) striking atoms and molecules of the high atmosphere as they plunge earthward along field lines of the Earth's magnetism. What was not known until recently—and some of the knowledge remains tentative—was the origin of these particles and how they achieve their extremely high energy and high speed—close to that of light.

Once the zones of most frequent auroras had been mapped on a global scale, a link to the Earth's magnetic field became apparent. It had early been observed that there are also southern lights—the aurora australis—in a zone encircling the South Pole, matching the one in the north. One of the international objectives of the First Polar Year in 1882–83 was to conduct simultaneous observations in both regions. Germany sent an expedition to South Georgia, near the Antarctic. French scientists went to Cape Horn. A dozen expeditions were dispatched to sites in the Arctic, including the ill-fated one led by Adolphus W. Greely. Only seven of its twenty-five members survived.

A half-century later the Second Polar Year was severely handicapped by the Great Depression, and it was not until the International Geophysical Year of 1957–58 that truly global observations were made, including the first from space. These led to discovery of the Van Allen radiation belts that encircle the Earth in space and made it possible to map the region in nearby space dominated by the Earth's magnetic field—the magnetosphere.

The recent reappearance of Halley's comet has made us particularly aware of the solar wind, a constant stream of very high-velocity gas blowing out in all directions from the sun. It is this solar wind that is chiefly responsible for forming comet tails and causing them invariably to point away from the sun. The solar wind also blows against the Earth's magnetic envelope, which otherwise would be shaped like an apple, with deep indentations over both poles. The wind, however, drags out part of this envelope to form a long tail like the wake extending far downstream

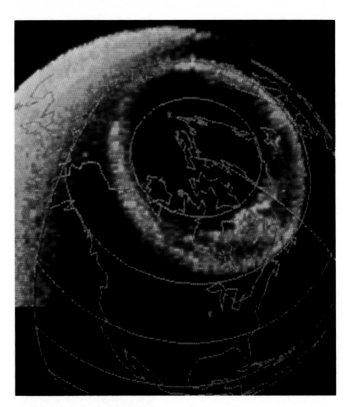

At ultraviolet wavelengths, an intense auroral emission following an interplanetary shock rivals emissions from the sunlight hemisphere (upper left portion of the image, obtained by University of Iowa via Dynamics Explorer 1).

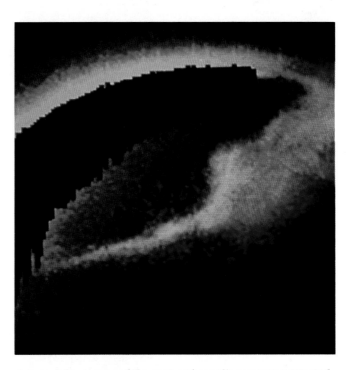

A true-color image of the aurora borealis was reconstructed at the University of Iowa Department of Physics and Astronomy from images received from the spacecraft Dynamics Explorer 1.

"Displays are classified into rays, pleated curtains, uniform glows (usually pink), and other forms. They can be almost incredibly dynamic, when one considers the size of the stage on which they are performing."

from a rock in a swift-flowing rapids. It is in the indented region—the stem and flower ends of the apple—that the particles causing the aurora plunge toward the Earth along the outermost shell of the Earth's magnetic field—the skin of the apple. From a variety of satellite observations it appears that the auroral particles gain much of their tremendous velocity where the solar wind sweeps past the magnetic tail. The particles are then channeled back toward the Earth from the outer part of the tail into the polar regions.

Within the last year or two, images obtained from spacecraft have shown that the auroras in both polar regions occur with striking similarity and simultaneity, as though almost "two halves of the same apple."

At times the cascading of high-energy particles into the auroral zone may carry energy that is equivalent to a billion kilowatts. Not all of this is manifested in visual displays. An intense electric current is generated in the auroral zone—the polar electrojet—that may induce voltages in long electric conductors on the Earth, such as powerlines and pipelines. It is calculated that one volt per kilometer can be induced in such a conductor. Provisions must be made to avoid transmission line overload. For the pipeline linking oil

fields on the North Slope of Alaska with the terminal at Valdez this would amount to about 600 volts, accelerating corrosion if the pipeline were not grounded.

Solar flares, or sunspots—great eruptions on the surface of the sun—distort the magnetic field of the Earth and cause the auroral zones to move farther from the poles. It is at these times that the northern lights can be seen south of the Canadian border. Even when the sun is near the low point of its eleven-year cycle of sunspots, the lights can be seen. Though we are not aware of them, auroras also form on the sunlit side of the auroral zone, joining with the nighttime display to form a complete circle. This was discovered in 1983 in images recorded by HILAT, the High Latitude Satellite. Its scanner was sensitive to ultraviolet light that made the display visible despite daylight.

The auroral zone is not centered on the North Pole, or even on the North Magnetic Pole. It remains roughly fixed relative to the direction of the sun. In Fairbanks, Alaska, at midnight, its southernmost part is directly overhead. Twelve hours later rotation of the Earth has placed that same sector of the circle over Iceland and the coast of Norway.

The displays occur between sixty and two

The aurora borealis is generated when electrically charged particles from the solar wind enter the Earth's magnetic field. This field, on the side away from the sun, is drawn out into a long tail by the force of the solar wind. Solar particles penetrate the magnetic field as the wind sweeps along the tail, perhaps a million miles long. The particles then travel back to Earth's polar regions, gaining speed and energy and generating an intense electric current. This current (inset) flows toward the Earth on the morning side and away from it on the evening side, forming the auroral lights.

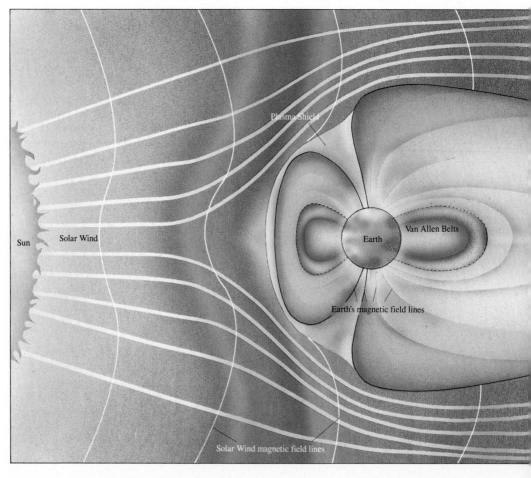

hundred miles above the Earth, their colors being determined by the nature of the atoms or molecules hit by incoming electrons and by the energies of those collisions. Molecules of oxygen, for example, glow red or green. Hydrogen molecules may likewise produce a red glow, whereas individual hydrogen atoms will radiate green light. Nitrogen atoms generate purple, and nitrogen molecules glow pink.

Displays are classified into rays, pleated curtains, uniform glows (usually pink), and other forms. They can be almost incredibly dynamic, when one considers the size of the stage on which they are performing. In February 1958 there was a particularly dramatic display. Even in cloudy areas of the United States the clouds took on an eerie red hue. If human bodies could sense magnetism, a large percentage of the Earth's inhabitants would have experienced a sensation akin to dizziness. Great electric currents were induced in the Earth. Lights flickered in farmhouses from Montana to Minnesota. Toronto and its environs were blacked out as currents tripped the utility circuit breakers.

Displays tend to reach their peak near midnight. If a display has been forecast, based on the occurrence of sunspots, to re-

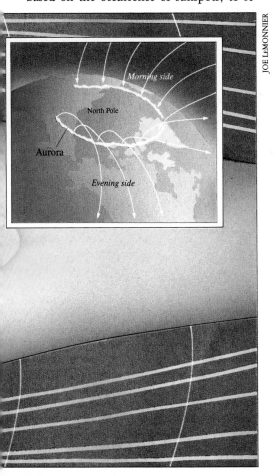

main abed could mean missing one of life's most thrilling experiences. Syun-Ichi Akasofu of the University of Alaska, one of the world's leading authorities on the aurora, likens the displays to television shows on a monumental scale. Under magnetic control, he points out, the incoming electrons illuminate the high atmosphere in much the same way as does the magnetically controlled beam of electrons falling on a TV screen.

A number of recently launched spacecraft have enlarged our knowledge and understanding of the aurora. In addition to HILAT, which has shown that displays occur as often on the sunlit side of the planet as on the night side, Dynamics Explorer 1, far enough out in space to view the entire Earth at once, has photographed auroras over both poles simultaneously. It has been recording small auroral events about twice a day, as well as a large "storm" once every four to six weeks.

When International Sun–Earth Explorer 3 was commanded in 1983 to leave its station between Earth and the sun to take a close look at the comet Giacobini–Zinner, its path wove in and out of the Earth's magnetotail for 850,000 miles. Its observations and those of IMP 8 (Interplanetary Monitoring Platform 8) have encouraged the belief that at least part of the auroral acceleration process occurs far back along the tail.

To explore how atomic particles from the sun can break through the Earth's magnetic envelope, prior to generating an aurora, a West German satellite released a tracer substance—lithium—into the solar wind before it encountered the Earth's magnetosphere. Inside that magnetosphere an American satellite watched for traces of this lithium but found none. However, at least some of the auroral particles come from the solar wind, because auroral displays are known to contain helium atoms that have been stripped of electrons by their earlier proximity to the sun's fiery furnace.

Perhaps, then, the solar wind penetrates into the tail, rather than where it hits the magnetosphere head on. It is clear that, despite all that has been learned and observed since the days of Lomonosov, a full understanding of those glorious curtains of light is not yet in sight.

WHERE A HEAVY BODY IS LIKELY TO SINK

TEXT BY WALTER HENRICKS HODGE

"The word 'bog' comes from the ancient Celtic language and means 'something soft that bends or sinks.'" Next page: The eye of a bog, a yellow pond lily, and sphagnum mat. "Each stage in bog succession exists as a band of different plants forming concentric rings around the open water."

Anyone who has enjoyed the Great North Woods has probably seen a sphagnum bog. For countless bogs associated with equally countless lakes and ponds are typical of that land of conifers, of low relief, slow streams, and shallow acid soils.

The great continental ice sheet which bulldozed and scoured the land during the Pleistocene era produced all of these characteristic features of a glaciated landscape. Subsequently, during the glacial retreat, a host of small basins and depressions were created, either gouged from the ground or formed where great fragments or bergs of ice were left behind in the ground to melt. Today these water-filled and poorly drained basins are the bogs, bog ponds, and so-called muskeg of the Great North Woods. In North America a line drawn from New York City to Chicago roughly delineates the location of the southernmost edge of our last continental glacier. Bogs and their associated ponds, common in the North, rarely occur below that line.

Bogs are unique among wetland communities in their lack of drainage. There are no inflowing or outflowing streams. Thus bog-pond water lacks dissolved air. This deficiency causes carbon dioxide to accumulate in the water, which inhibits the growth of the microscopic flora characteristic of well-drained lakes and ponds. Normally included in this aquatic flora are important bacteria and fungi which, as the major agents of decomposition, feed upon dead or dying matter. Lack of these important decomposer organisms means that the process of decay in a bog is practically nonexistent and dead vegetation accumulates in large quantities to form peat. At the same time the bog water and the soils permeated by it become highly acid. Relatively few plants can tolerate such acidic conditions. Those that do comprise a small but unique fraternity, including special mosses, unusual herbaceous plants, a little group of boreal shrubs, and two notable trees.

As with the plants, the animal life—especially that of more northern bogs—tends to lack variety. Certain bog features serve as natural barriers for some animals. Fish, for example, are few or nonexistent; the absence of a drainage system of streams in bog ponds efficiently bars fish migration. This barrier is no problem to amphibians or reptiles, and the *chug-a-rum* of the bullfrog or the splash of an occasional turtle are sounds that punctuate the quiet solitude of a bog in summer. Certainly there is no dearth of flying creatures, primarily insects but also birds, which find bogs to be ideal hidden havens. These suit not only waterfowl but many kinds of songbirds, especially those species that claim the northern boreal forest as their home. Of mammals, deer and moose are also visitors, but for them the bog is a mixed blessing: Its wooded margins offer them protected sanctuary in summer though, at the same time, the unstable sphagnum mat bars these heavy animals from their favorite food—the water lilies that are so prevalent in bog-pond shallows.

Abundant though they are, bogs are less frequented by the casual visitor than are other wetland communities. The word "bog" comes from the ancient Celtic language and means "something soft that bends or sinks." Perhaps our general unfamiliarity with these interesting habitats stems from an innate fear that a bog is, as Webster defines, "wet spongy ground where a heavy body is likely to sink."

Bogs are not quagmires. Rather than being places to shun, they have much of interest to offer the lover of nature. Besides the chance to see some rather unusual plants, a bog offers one of the best sites to observe how plant growth can eventually transform the open water of a pond into a mature forest of conifers. The plant ecologist calls this natural metamorphosis "succession."

In the Northeast, late June or early July is an excellent time to explore a bog. Then the blackflies are mostly gone and some of the showier bog wildflowers may be in bloom. You should pick a bog that still possesses some open water, for then all successional stages can be observed.

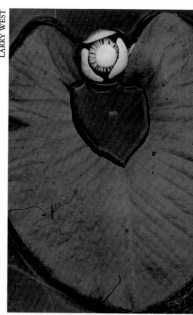

The approach to a bog usually is through the local climax forest. In Canada, and certain of our bordering states, it is the boreal forest of conifers. Farther south, in the northeastern states, mature deciduous forest is the rule. These are the forests which, if the land lies undisturbed by man, will ultimately dominate the scene. The bog, too, will in time become filled in and disappear, to be occupied by mature forest.

As we step through the fringes of mature forest adjacent to the bog, we will be on the outer edge of the original glacial pond, now transformed to forest. Here the forest is in transition. Groups of mature climax trees,

A sampling of abundant bog life: a midge (top right), bog copper butterfly (top left), an insect-devouring pitcher plant (above). Also a fly is trapped by a sundew, and a dragonfly pauses.

occupying more solid ground, are often interspersed with damp, sphagnum-filled glades. Beneath the trees grow some of the familiar spring wildflowers of the North Woods—goldthread, starflower, and wood sorrel—while in wetter places there are often clumps of cinnamon fern. But these plants are not the bog species we have come to see. Like the trees, they are a part of the climax community that is waiting patiently to occupy the bog once it fills in and becomes dry land.

Farther in, we encounter two conifers—black (or bog) spruce and tamarack—whose presence is a sure sign that we are now on the bog itself. Tamarack, or American larch, is a true boreal species. This small tree grows farther north than any other save for the creeping Arctic willows. Like them, but unlike most conifers, tamarack drops its needle-leaves in winter. Then "it is the deadest looking vegetation on the globe" in the words of the late Donald Culross Peattie, who added that in spring "there is no more delicate charm in the North Woods than the moment when the soft, pale-green needles first begin to clothe the military sternness of the larch. So fine is that foliage, and so oddly clustered in sparse tufts, that tamarack has the distinction among our trees of giving the least shade." Though abundant throughout the boreal forest, tamarack seems to prefer bogs and muskeg. Indeed, at the southern part of its range—which coincides with the southernmost extent of glacial ice during Pleistocene times—native stands of tamarack can only be found in sphagnum bogs.

Bog water seems to impart a special strength to the wood of tamarack. Indians collected its tough, pliant rootlets to serve as thread for joining strips of birchbark on their canoes, and the durable wood is still used by the white man in fashioning the knees, keels, and flooring of small craft.

The tamarack's constant associate in bogs, the black or bog spruce, has a similar geographical range. However, unlike the tamarack, black spruce grows into a fine forest tree on other than bog soil. But then it becomes the prey of the lumberman, who logs it, along with the more abundant white spruce, for its fine pulpwood. In the refuge of the bog, unnaturally dwarfed by unsteady footing for its roots, the black spruce attracts no woodcutter. Nor does it attract—in these days of synthetic chewing gum—the collectors who nearly a century ago sought spruce gum, a resinous exudate that is produced regularly on the surface of black spruce bark. Bog spruce still produces its gum. Pluck off a bit and sample what once

was the standard chewing gum of the old North Woods lumber camps.

Black spruce foliage, too, produced spruce beer, a once popular beverage, described by Thoreau in his *Maine Woods* as a "lumberer's drink, which would acclimate and naturalize a man at once—which would make him see green, and, if he slept, dream that he heard the wind sough among the pines."

As we push through the fringing trees of tamarack and spruce toward the open area of the bog, we find that the individual conifers rapidly decrease in size until they are scarcely breast height. Presently we are beyond the point where bog trees can grow. Here the open water forming the "eye," the center of the bog, is clearly visible, perhaps a hundred feet distant. This is the best spot to stop and observe the several stages in bog succession. Each stage exists as a band of different plants forming concentric rings around the open water. The first ring is of pioneering aquatic plants, with floating leaves. They include white water lilies and the less showy yellow spatterdock with its globular, petal-less blossoms. At the water's edge is the second ring, composed of shallow water herbs. This stage is dominated usually by an assortment of sedges, often accompanied by the widespread bogbean *(Menyanthes),* no bean at all but rather a member of the gentian family. Like those of the neighboring water lilies, the thick rootstocks of the bogbean are starch-filled and edible, and have long been used in Scandinavia for making bitter-tasting *missen* bread (famine bread), described by the Finns and Lapps as "thoroughly unpalatable but nonetheless nutritious."

Between the waterline community and the edge of the bog tree zone lies the third successional stage. It is occupied by mounds of sphagnum moss forming a mat that is interspersed with a variety of herbs and low shrubs. Sometimes the latter form a separate outer ring adjacent to the belt of bog trees, the next-to-last step in bog succession leading to the final climax. In northern bogs the most interesting and greatest variety of plants occupy the mat of sphagnum.

Now the bog begins to live up to Webster's definition. Our feet sink at each step into inches of cool water. A jump makes the matted vegetation undulate and sway for yards around. We are now on the quaking part of the bog. This is a buoyant floating mat composed of several species of the gray-green mosses called sphagnum. The mat is held together and strengthened by the interlaced roots and creeping branches of the small shrubs and herbs that call it their home. Thus the mat, which may become one

JOHN SHAW

A dried pitcher plant flower. A recent emigrant from southern regions, where it is now rare, the common pitcher plant has spread across the boreal belt because it is able to survive intense winters.

109

The staminate flower of a tamarack (top left), an ancient spruce laden with lichens (right), and two lovely representatives of the bog orchid community—an arethusa (top right) and a yellow-fringed orchid. "In few places outside the tropics can one see the variety of orchids to be found on a bog. As many as fourteen kinds have been recorded on a bog less than an acre in size."

to two feet thick, is a natural floating garden that extends out over the surface waters of the pond. From the mat it would be hard to touch the oozy bottom with the proverbial ten-foot pole.

Now one can understand why the transition between the mat and the bog trees is so marked. Tamarack and spruce need terra firma for their deep, probing roots, and they find it nearly impossible to grow on the mat—at least not until solid ground is finally built up beneath it.

Watch your step on a quaking bog. Inevitably feet get wet, but one can limit it to that. A good technique for quaking bog explorers is to step only where there are patches of shrubs, avoiding bare mounds of sphagnum, where the mat may be weaker.

Sphagnum mosses are remarkable plants. The rapid growth and subsequent decay of these lowly mosses assure the conversion of ponds to bogs and eventually to climax forest. Once the moss becomes established as a ring around the pond margins, it grows steadily out over the water to form the quaking mat. The water surface becomes sealed over completely. During the process there is a constant fall of detritus from shed leaves, stems, and the like. This material piles up on the pond bottom to form deposits of peat, which is nothing more than partially decayed plant matter. Eventually the peat will fill the old pond basin completely. The time required to convert an open pond into bog or muskeg may be relatively short. Some northern lakes shown on maps made a century ago are now bogs. Perhaps in another century or two, if succession is left to nature, new maps will show only mature forest.

The acidic pond water that overlies and permeates peat has proven to be nature's best embalming fluid. Anything dead, plant or animal, tends to be well-preserved when it falls into the bed of a bog pond. So-called "bogwood"—actually waterlogged trunks of centuries-old trees that have been buried in peat—is often mined to produce excellent lumber. Wonderfully preserved human bodies, millennia old, complete with clothing and burial artifacts, have been excavated from Danish bogs during peat-mining operations. Even more remarkable were seeds of sacred lotus *(Nelumbo nucifera)*, an aquatic plant, which a Japanese scientist found buried in a Manchurian peat bog. The hard, thick seed coats of the lotus make it unusually long-lived. When radiocarbon dating demonstrated the seeds to be 2,000 years old, it was hardly expected that they would germinate. Yet when planted every one grew, making this apparently the longest period of

dormancy yet recorded for a living thing.

The presence of lotus seeds in a Manchurian bog shows that the species was once a member of that bog's aquatic flora. In fact, all peat bog deposits yield up valuable clues concerning changes in climate and in associated plant populations during the many years that have passed since the last great glacial period. Well-preserved and hence identifiable plant materials of all types, especially wind-dispersed pollens, are deposited annually in bog ponds. Thus ecologists need only make and study cores of a bog's sediments to determine the types of plants that were growing in that area over thousands of years.

Having seen what peat mosses can do in the process of plant succession, let's look at the moss itself. Most of the three hundred or more sphagnum species grow only in boggy soft-water sites where little lime is present. To the layman most of these mosses look alike, yet several kinds may be found on a typical northern bog. Each species occupies its own special bog niche. Sphagnums differ from other mosses in the unique form of their leaves as well as in their characteristic gray-green color. At times the rosette-like growing tips are pink or red, making them look almost like flowers. In midsummer the rosettes sport tiny, black, ball-like structures. These represent the spore-producing generation that—as in all mosses—remains permanently attached as a parasite to the mother plant. Spores shed by these curious parasites produce a new sexual generation of moss.

Under a lens one sees that the pale color of sphagnum is due to the presence of a large proportion of water-absorbing cells. These lack the green pigment, chlorophyll, found in the adjacent photosynthetic cells. The unique colorless cells enable sphagnum to absorb and store enormous amounts of water, as much as sixteen or eighteen times its own weight. Such large quantities are required to power the plant's profligate growth.

It is this water-holding capacity that makes dried sphagnum and its by-product, peat moss, so important in horticulture. There it serves as a mulch and improver of tilth. Moreover, seedlings germinated in sphagnum, a sterile medium, do not suffer from attacks of "damping-off" fungi that invade plants near the ground and cause wilting. The innate antiseptic properties of sphagnum, combined with its great absorbency, made it popular centuries ago as a surgical dressing. The Japanese used it on a large scale a hundred years ago in their war with Russia. Wounds dressed with sphagnum

This page: leatherleaf (below) ablaze in October, and the flowers of bogbean, a member of the gentian family whose rootstock is used by Finns and Lapps to make a bitter-tasting bread. Next page: an assortment of sedges, including cottongrass, which dominates the plant community at a bog's waterline. The two top photos are of sphagnum mat, where "our feet sink at each step into inches of cool water... In midsummer the rosettes sport tiny, black, ball-like structures. These represent the spore-producing generation that remains attached as a parasite to the mother plant."

LES LINE

LES LINE

were invariably found to be in better condition than when cotton was used—even when the dressings were left unattended for nearly two weeks.

Of all the plants that call a bog their home, by far the greatest number share the quaking mat with the sphagnum. Most of these species are so typical of bogs that one must visit a bog in order to see them. These include a handful of small evergreen shrubs —all members of the heath family—plus a coterie of herbaceous plants, of which the cotton grasses, bog orchids, and certain insectivorous species are the most conspicuous. All share—along with the pioneering trees— the ability to live where the groundwater is normally highly acid.

Like the tamarack and spruce, the shrubby heaths are boreal plants that abound in the universally cool lands of the taiga, the conifer forest that rings all northern continents just south of the tundra. There, they may occupy well-drained soil as well as bogs. But south of the boreal belt, in the northeastern and north-central United States, the cool, acidic growing conditions of the boreal forest are seldom found except in the bog community. There, air, soil, and water temperatures are always noticeably cooler than in surrounding areas. Apparently the rapid water transpiration from the sphagnum leaves functions as a kind of natural air-conditioner. In addition, the thick floating mat provides an insulating layer, keeping the pond water beneath it continually cool and largely unaffected by the warming rays of the summer sun.

Man has recognized the natural habitat of the heaths by giving them such names as bog rosemary (Andromeda), bog laurel (Kalmia), and bog tea (Ledum). All of them are low, unprepossessing shrubs, seldom more than a foot or two high. Even more inconspicuous are the vinelike cranberries, whose creeping stems are easily overlooked until autumn, when their berries brighten the sphagnum with red.

If judged by its abundance, leatherleaf (Chamaedaphne) is the most successful of the heaths. Its branches root readily at their nodes, enabling it to spread quickly over the mat to form large colonies. Leatherleaf is also the earliest of the heaths to flower, its white pendant blossoms opening in early May, well before other bog plants have developed new leaves. In autumn, leatherleaf's leaves, turned red, enliven the bog with color.

In their form and structure, the leaves of heaths reflect the problems of life in a bog. All have a similar look and shape, quite unlike the leaves of shrubs living outside the bog community. Mostly elliptical, they tend

to be thick and leathery. Often their edges are strongly inrolled, and the lower surface may contain dense wool, as in bog tea, or the whitish waxy bloom of bog rosemary and bog laurel. All such leaf structures serve against water loss and subsequent wilting, and are most frequently associated with desert plants. But why such modifications on bog shrubs? In a way, acid bogs are much like deserts, at least as far as plants are concerned. For even though there is plenty of water, it is so highly acid that plant roots cannot readily absorb it. In the desert, freshwater is largely physically absent and unavailable to plants. In a bog, water is, physiologically speaking, also unavailable to the freshwater-seeking roots of plants. Our bog, botanists would say, because of its acidic water, is a physiological desert, and the bog shrub leaves demonstrate this fact in both form and structure.

Despite the water problem, the heaths are able to thrive and flower. The majority produce rather inconspicuous blossoms, resembling those of their cousin blueberries, with which they are often associated. Perhaps the showiest are the clustered white trusses of bog tea, which bloom in early summer. Most colorful are the rosy-purple blooms of bog laurel. Most charming are those of the cranberries; the pink reflexed petals and yellow stamens look like miniatures of the flowers of our western shooting stars.

Of all the world's bog species only one, the big-fruited American cranberry, has been tapped by man to join the select group of his domesticated plants. The cranberry is also the only one of a handful of crop plants—including the sunflower, blueberry, and pecan—that actually originated within the boundaries of what is now the United States.

113

In cultivation for less than a century, this newcomer is a babe-in-arms compared with man's other Stone Age crops. Modern cranberry cultivars are productive strains selected from the wild but grown on the same kind of bog habitat that was their original home. Fully mature bogs are simply cleared, leveled, and drained—to be reflooded as required for cranberry monoculture. At time of harvest, growers have adopted the cranberry's normal method of seed dispersal, flotation, to gather the crop. Following bog flooding, special machines strip the submerged vines of their berries, which then bob to the surface to form colorful floating windrows that are promptly collected for processing.

The floating sphagnum mat is famed for its interesting orchids. Indeed in few places outside the tropics can one see the variety often to be found on a bog. As many as fourteen kinds have been recorded on a bog less than an acre in size. Doubtless the count included such typical species as rose pogonia *(Pogonia)*, swamp and grass pinks *(Arethusa* and *Calopogon)*, ladies tresses *(Spiranthes)*, and a selection of fringed orchids *(Habenaria)* and ladyslippers *(Cypripedium)*.

Some of these orchids are not limited to bogs but occur elsewhere in quite unboglike sites. Their presence in bogs relates to the fact that bogs are often the only undisturbed refuges left for such acid-loving species, and also may be the only acidic habitats in areas where most soils are either neutral or alkaline.

Scientists have learned that orchids—and heaths—thrive in acid soils because of a special relationship that exists between the roots of these plants and specialized "acid-loving" soil fungi, called *mycorrhizae* (literally "fungus roots"). These strange fungi live symbiotically upon or within the feeding roots of orchids, decomposing and assimilating organic materials in the acid soil and sharing the food with their hosts in return for a "home." Thus the fungi and not the orchids are the ones that require acid soil in which to prosper. On the other hand, so close is the communal relationship that orchids and heaths cannot live without their mycorrhizal guests.

The fungus-orchid relationship has proven so successful that on some bogs certain orchids may form colonies numbering in the thousands. Such colonies are more typical of the cool spruce-tamarack bogs that abound around the Great Lakes states. The showy ladyslipper, queen of northern orchids and one of America's most popular wildflowers, is especially known for such breathtaking displays. Seeing it in full bloom in sphagnum openings under the half-shade of the bog conifers, one can easily understand why Minnesota has adopted this charmer as its state flower. No other native orchid has been so honored.

In such sylvan glades, this big pink-and-white slipper orchid is often joined by the yellow ladyslipper, one of the very few orchids with worldwide distribution in the boreal belt. Curiously, the yellow ladyslipper has two forms. One sports small slippers; those of the other are much larger. But be cautious with this orchid trio: their leaves, covered with soft glandular hairs, are poisonous and if touched can cause severe dermatitis, just like poison ivy.

Unlike the ladyslippers, most bog orchids prefer the full sun of the quaking bog. There one can find an early flowering trio of showy rose-colored orchids—grass pink, rose pogonia, and swamp pink. Later, in the summer, the fringed orchids, or habenarias, appear. They take their name from the delicately fringed margins of the prominent orchid "lip" petal. The showier habenarias—with numerous white flowers on erect racemes—are sometimes as populous on the sunny sphagnum mat as the ladyslippers are in the shade. Other habenarias, like the solitary greenish-flowered frog orchids, though common, are inconspicuous and hard to find. To the layman these insignificant little plants hardly fulfill their concept of what an orchid should be.

Plants that can turn the tables on insects by eating them—instead of the reverse—always evoke interest. Several kinds of insectivorous plants are as common on bogs as are the orchids, with which they fraternize. They include the common pitcher plant *(Sarracenia purpurea)* and several species of the insignificant sundews *(Drosera)*. Unlike the bog orchids, which are conspicuous only when in flower, the insect-catchers have colorful leaves and thus are visible to the visitor throughout the growing season.

The nitrogen-deficient bog soil poses no problem to these plants. Raw materials for food are derived from the nitrogen-rich bodies of the insects they capture. Leaves rather than roots perform the task of taking in the nutrients required for photosynthesis. Thus the root systems of insectivorous plants tend to be weak and rather poorly developed. The acid bog water doesn't bother them, for they function almost solely for support.

The little sundews, with their worldwide distribution, are the most numerous and apparently the most successful of all insectivorous plants. It is not surprising to find

114

"The showy ladyslipper, queen of northern orchids and one of America's most popular wildflowers."

several kinds making their home in the sphagnum mat. Despite their abundance, sundews are often overlooked. But one can often spot colonies where the sphagnum is thin or where there are patches of bare soil.

A close look at a sundew plant reveals a small rosette of spoon-shaped leaves covered completely with long reddish hairs. Atop each hair is a gland that secretes a globule of sticky "sun dew." In the sun the whole plant appears to light up, forming an attractive beacon to unwary prey. The prey of the sundew leaf consists of tiny gnats, midges, and mosquitoes.

Woe betide any gnat that lands on the glistening orb, for it is promptly ensnared by on ̄ of nature's original flypapers. Reacting to the insect's weight, the hairs operate like tentacles, bending slowly about the prey, smothering it, and eventually forcing the victim against the sensitive surface of the leaf. The leaf then bends imperceptibly like a fist to grasp the prey. Subsequently a digestive ferment appears and its activity results ultimately in the complete assimilation of the food. Once the meal is completed, the leaf again expands, producing a new glob of sticky sun dew for another catch. The whole cycle of capture, digestion, assimilation, and trap resetting may take several days.

The evolution of what Charles Darwin called an "incredible and wonderful" leaf trap has enabled sundews to thrive and reproduce, in spite of the nitrogen-deficient soils in which they are rooted. Their little inflorescences appear throughout the summer. The white flowers open one at a time, and then only briefly when the sun is at its fullest.

Fast-growing sphagnum often overwhelms and smothers the little annual sundews. They are then replaced by the other insect-catcher of the northern bog, the common pitcher plant, also known as huntsman's cup and sidesaddle flower.

Pitcher plants are among the largest of insectivorous plants. Their leaf rosettes readily attract the visitor's eye as brilliant splashes of red, spotted here and there throughout the bog. They give the impression of flowers, and so they must appear to insects on the lookout for pollen and nectar.

The pitcher plant trap is operated in quite a different fashion from that of the sundew. It is a passive rather than an active one. Prey initially lured by the flower-like color encounter a rosette of semi-erect tubular leaves filled at least partially with rainwater. Since they are consequently heavy, the thick growth of the surrounding moss serves as packing, helping to support and keep them erect. The extremity of each leaf is expanded, forming a convenient landing pad, while special nectar glands ring the pitcher mouth. Thus the enticing lure of honey must convince an approaching insect that the colorful leaf is really a flower. The landing pad itself has an ingenious design that permits it to serve as a sort of one-way street. The short, stiff hairs that cover its surface all point in one direction—inward, toward the pitcher mouth with its seductive smell of nectar. Within the leaf funnel, beyond the orifice, are additional down-pointing hairs, as well as a slick "slide zone," devoid of hairs. This combination of remarkable modifications assures the plant of continual trapping success. Insects invariably fall into the watery cisterns and are drowned. It is easy to see how the pitcher traps function. Just cut off and slit open an older leaf. Within, you are sure to find a mass of decomposing insect bodies. As with the sundew, the decaying mass yields a nitrogen-rich gruel that is soon assimilated by special cells at the base of the leaf.

For a short period, usually in mid-June, pitcher plants burst into purplish bloom. Then the bog is decorated with their unusual globular blossoms, which match those of the orchids in showiness. The curious fiddle-shaped petals soon fall, but the leathery calyx and umbrella-like style persist until the seeds mature.

All pitcher plants of the genus *Sarracenia* are native to eastern North America. Most of the ten species occur in a limited area in and about northern Florida. Botanists believe that is their place of origin. So the common pitcher plant that is abundant in bogs from Labrador to Minnesota and Saskatchewan is actually a newcomer to the North Woods country, an emigrant from much farther south. Its wanderings demonstrate how and why certain plants have been able to migrate in post-Pleistocene times.

Several species of *Sarracenia* more resistant to cold than the others have been able to migrate slowly northward along the Atlantic coastal plain. But only one, the common pitcher plant, proved able to survive the intense winters much farther north; its leaf rosettes are regularly frozen solid during the winter months when all the bog is turned to ice. This tolerance to cold permitted the species to expand its original range greatly, for as it moved northward it suddenly found a land of endless bogs in the recently glaciated north country. Conditions for growth were so ideal that a population explosion of pitcher plants resulted. Today *Sarracenia purpurea* is a rare plant in its old home area, where most of the few bogs that existed have been destroyed by man. On the other hand, in the boreal bogs of the largely virgin taiga the pitcher plant numbers are legion. Botanists now believe that if the pitcher plant is given sufficient time, it may eventually populate the whole boreal belt of bogs around the world.

Like *Sarracenia,* all the plants in its close-knit community have had to migrate, jumping from bog to bog, often over long distances of inhospitable land. Yet whatever sphagnum mat is visited, whether in the Maine woods or the Lake Superior wilderness, one thing is certain; the plants—whether tree, shrub, herb, or moss—will be essentially the same. It seems then that the methods nature has evolved for dispersing these species, whether by wind, water, or other living creatures, have been eminently successful. And so the fun of making one's way carefully out onto a mat of quaking sphagnum, "where a heavy body is likely to sink," is to find and enjoy unusual plants to be seen nowhere else.

LARRY WEST

Above, the olive-sided flycatcher whistles a familiar demand in northern boglands: "quick-three-beers." Opposite page: The cup nest of a hermit thrush may be found in a bed of moss beneath the climax trees surrounding the bog.

JOHN SHAW

VI
WILD PLANTS AND MAN

Billy the Kid was born in a New York slum, his sixgun and rifle were made in Connecticut, and the best covered wagons were built in Concord, New Hampshire. Which doesn't mean such products were eastern. Some things only start in the East, and really come into their own farther west.

Take cottonwoods.

There were always cottonwoods of one breed or another through much of the East and South, though they were never really appreciated there. Other trees were as big, and most had better wood. Being a cottonwood in an eastern forest was being a ninety-foot weed.

But all that changed out toward the 100th Meridian, out in the great grasslands where most eastern trees faded and failed, dying of wind, thirst, and general loneliness out along the buffalo rivers. There the cottonwood didn't suffer by comparison with the lordly oaks, beeches, chestnuts, and tulip trees of the Wooden States. It was enough that it was a tree, thick-boled and broad-limbed, breaking the infinite sweep of sky and grass and signifying shade, firewood, and water in a land that was notably lacking in all three.

In his 1859 *Hand Book for Overland Expeditions* Captain Randolph Marcy advised: "There are many indications of water known to old campaigners, although none of them are absolutely infallible. The most certain of them are deep-green cottonwood or willow trees growing in depressed localities..." And although these cottonwood groves were near water, they rarely exhaled evil vapors. Captain Marcy happily revealed that "the streams which intersect our great prairies have but a very sparse growth of wood or vegetation upon their banks, so that one of the fundamental causes for the generation of noxious malaria does not, to any great extent, exist here, and I believe that persons may encamp with impunity directly upon their banks."

With alacrity, too. For the deeper the wagon trains rolled into the West and summer, the more intense and prolonged the relentless sun that shrank wheel rims and spokes, bleaching the wagon-covers like snow even while it darkened the faces and hands of women who had prided themselves on pale gentility, falling in a heavy, monotonous flood of light on a land that lay stunned and silent under its weight. Consider, then, fac-

WEST BEGINS

TEXT BY JOHN MADSON

·

PHOTOGRAPHY BY STEPHEN TRIMBLE

Plains cottonwoods on the site of Teddy Roosevelt's Maltese Cross Ranch, in North Dakota.

The leaves of a Plains cottonwood are fringed with down from fruiting catkins. "The tree was closely bound to many parts of tribal life; the Sundance Lodge was often made of cottonwood saplings, and in the Snake and Antelope dances the chief priest might wear a chaplet of cottonwood leaves. Indian children made toy tepees of the leaves, arranging them in circles like the camp of their own band."

ing into the deep blaze of late afternoon, already spent from ten hours of travel, and cresting a prairie ridge to see that dark-green line of trees in the middle distance. Wood for cooking just ahead, with supper tonight under a green leaf canopy and fireside fiddles after. Trees shutting out those endless horizons, with water for the livestock, for the barrels, for bathing. A green and restful place set about with fine cottonwood trees, the little prairie creek running sweet and clear in the dappled shade. Heaven enough, for now.

Years after, the sons of some of those travelers made new routes as they took the first trail herds north and east. And even though these cowboys had been bred to sun and sky in this land with its jarring excesses of light, they still cherished a shady nooning under cottonwoods—and they wove it into an old night-herding song, "The Railroad Corral":

> *Now the sun circles upward;*
> *The steers as they plod*
> *Are poundin' to powder*
> *The hot prairie sod.*
> *It seems as the dust*
> *Makes you dizzy and sick,*
> *That we'll never reach noon*
> *And a cool shady crick.*

That crick was likely shaded by some boxelder, and maybe green ash and black willow. And cottonwood—always cottonwood. The cowboy boiled his Arbuckle coffee with it, fried his beefsteak over it, built corrals and line shacks and ranch buildings of it, and used it to heat branding irons. If one of those happened to be a running iron used too freely on someone else's stock, the cottonwood might also be a hanging tree. And for rustler and honest drover alike, a cottonwood might be the only lasting grave marker he'd ever have. When cowboy Andy Adams helped push a Texas herd over Doan's Crossing of the Red River in 1882 there were already five graves under the cottonwoods there—all of drovers who had drowned at the crossing in little more than a year. At Forty Islands Ford on the North Platte that summer, Andy would help bury a trail boss in still another cottonwood grove.

But long before any wagons and trail herds, the cottonwood rivers of the prairies and plains belonged to the Osages, Kiowas, Comanches, Arapaho, Pawnee, Crows, Arikaras, Mandans, Sioux, and Cheyenne. No one cherished good campsites more, and in all the grass country there were no finer than the riverside benches shaded with their evenly spaced groves of cottonwood trees.

Rich places, full and flowing. In 1840 the great Indian Peace Council was held in the groves of the Arkansas River just downstream from Bent's Fort in eastern Colorado—and there was grass, shade, water, and fuel enough for 5,000 Indians and over 8,000 horses.

Useful and comfortable in summer, the cottonwood camps were almost essential in winter. They provided about as much shelter as one could expect in that country, with plenty of firewood and that vital component of the buffalo hunter's economy: horse feed. The sweet inner bark of Plains cottonwood was relished by horses, and during George Custer's winter campaign of 1868–69 against Indians south of the Arkansas River, the mounts and pack animals in his command were often fed cottonwood bark. That winter he invariably found Indians camped along streams with heavy stands of cottonwood, the villages strewn with whitening branches that had been stripped of bark. In what must have otherwise been a pretty grim campaign, Custer was amused by Indian ponies feeding on cottonwood limbs that were cut into pieces about four feet long and thrown on the ground like any other fodder. A pony would put one hoof on a branch to hold it—something like a dog holding a bone—while gnawing the bark. "Although not affording anything like the amount of nutriment which either hay or grain does, yet our horses invariably preferred the bark to either, probably on account of its freshness," Custer reported.

The Plains tribes might use cottonwood root in making a fire with a friction drill—and then burn the bark to roast clays used in making cosmetic paints. In early spring yellow dye was made from the buds, and the bark might be stripped and the trunk scraped to obtain the sweet milky juice. The tree was closely bound to many parts of tribal life; the Sundance Lodge was often made of cottonwood saplings, and in the Snake and Antelope dances the chief priest might wear a chaplet of cottonwood leaves. Many of the drums and kachina dolls of the Pueblos are still carved of cottonwood.

Indian children made toy tepees of the leaves. A triangular cottonwood leaf was split a short distance from the tip down along the midrib. At equal distances from the leaf's tip a short tear was made across from each edge. The margin above each of these tears was bent back to simulate the smoke flaps of a tepee. The leaf margins below the tears were drawn together and fastened with a small thorn or splinter—and a tiny lodge was created. Children might make a number of these, arranging them in circles like the camp of their own band.

Settlers' children played with toys whittled from the corky bark that was up to three inches thick on old trees, and I know ranch women in the Nebraska Sandhills who create striking wall decorations with slabs of the deeply fissured bark. A little farther west, in the campgrounds of Devils Tower National Monument, cottonwood bark may be the only firewood available at the campsite. The first time we cooked over it I used words I hadn't thought of since high school—but the stuff wasn't so bad, at that. It takes a deal of starting, but it's smokeless and burns hot enough, leaves a talcum-fine ash, and has a little higher social status than buffalo chips.

Handy stuff, cottonwood bark. All kinds of uses. In parts of the Great Plains the water may be heavily charged with alkali and other harsh salts and can inflict the disorder that granddad called "the gypwater quickstep." It's an occupational hazard of cowboying, but on the trail its gastric pyrotechnics could be eased with snakeroot or other herbs—and sometimes cottonwood bark. Charles Goodnight, cattle king of the Texas Panhandle, recalled that cowboys "would get the inside bark, boil it to a strong tea, and drink liberally. It is a hell of a drink, a wonderful astringent, and a bitter dose. But it is a sure shot."

There weren't many real cowboys and Indians in my Iowa boyhood, but some of the dream kind rode through the upper stories of a vast cottonwood that grew only a few yards from the back porch where I slept. In the mid-watches of summer nights when the air was almost as heavy with humid heat as it had been at noon, a little night breeze might rise and set the cottonwood leaves ticking, and in my sweaty half-sleep the rattling leaves became a host of distant hooves, not in file order as a troop of cavalry might be, but unshod and coming on fast in the open order of painted war ponies. It was, after all, the same sort of tree that had heard the charges of Roman Nose's Cheyennes against Major Forsyth on Beecher's Island, and the sounds of Gall and Crazy Horse closing with Major Reno on the banks of the Greasy Grass. Perhaps cottonwoods never forget such sounds. Maybe they dream aloud on sultry summer nights when restive kids are just enough awake to hear them and enough asleep to understand. If this is so, pity the boys in their air-conditioned summer slumber, never hearing the night riders in the cottonwoods.

Then and now, the drainage systems of my Midwest are cottonwood country supreme. Here in the rich alluvial silts of river islands

and floodplains, the eastern cottonwood is at its proudest. It does best on moist, well-drained soils and rarely becomes a well-shaped tree on sites more than fifty feet above the average stream level of the area; on higher ground the cottonwood may assume a somewhat bushy appearance, its lowest limbs within easy reach. But under floodplain conditions the bole of an eastern cottonwood may rise sixty feet to the first limbs, attaining a height of 150 feet and a trunk diameter of seven feet or more on favorable sites west of

123

Barren branches of narrowleaf cottonwoods in fading winter light, and a blanket of fallen leaves from Rio Grande cottonwoods in a dry streambed. "Settlers are sometimes given credit for introducing cottonwoods to areas where none existed, even along certain treeless streams."

the Mississippi. One of the largest cottonwoods on record was eleven feet in diameter and 175 feet high.

Cottonwoods are among the giants of the floodplain forests of the Mississippi Valley, where only the pecan, sycamore, and some silver maples can challenge their girth and stature. The huge trees tower up out of fetid understories, raising lofty sunlit crowns that may support great blue heron rookeries that are seldom less than forty feet above the ground and sometimes occupy twenty acres of forest canopy. When such a rookery is "ripe" the upper levels of the cottonwoods and sycamores are a bedlam of harsh clucks, whoops, and rusty creakings. Far below, the unstirring air is so gray with whining mosquitoes that local folks say "you can reach out, close your hand, and leave a sort of white place hanging in the air."

Up into the huge trees climb the lianas—wild grape, moonseed, hog peanut, woodbine—the vines whose leaves may compose a fourth of the forest canopy. Here in this temperate jungle there is even an analog of the strangler fig, the heavy poison ivy vines that may be thicker than a man's arm, snaking up into the crowns of the tallest cottonwoods. Several of these massive vines may use one tree with branchings and rootings that can kill the tree by strangulation. The upper parts of such poison ivy lianas may develop a canopy almost as dense as that of the host tree, complete with strong horizontal branches, and long after the host has been strangled the heavy vines may be supported by the dead and whitening trunk as a sort of "poison-ivy tree." It's a hellish thing for anyone sensitive to it, and some of my river-rat friends refuse to hunt squirrels in bottom-

Narrowleaf cottonwoods in autumn splendor line a creek in Colorado's Great Sand Dunes National Monument.

land pecan groves because the bushytails sometimes hide in high clumps of poison ivy leaves. Woe to the man who handles such a squirrel with his bare hands.

For all their lowland preference, cottonwoods are surprisingly drought resistant. Although not found naturally on droughty soils, cottonwoods were planted extensively around homesteads by early settlers on the Plains, and once established they did well. Those settlers are sometimes given credit for introducing cottonwoods to areas where none existed, even along certain treeless streams. No one will ever know the straight of that. The early travelers on the Plains were forest-bred and usually thought of trees in terms of extensive woodlands of commercial saw timber. In their reports, land might be designated "prairie" even though it supported trees several feet in diameter. This way of looking at things may have been inspired by Zebulon Pike, who tended to regard the Plains as treeless desert even though there were trees large enough to be hewn into dugout canoes. (During the 1860s, the huge boles of Missouri River cottonwoods were sometimes used to make freight pirogues. Trunks as much as four feet thick were hollowed with fire and adze, and two of these lashed together could provide stable transport for up to fifteen tons.)

We'll never really know about the original prairie trees and how they were ranged by subspecies and ecology through the grasslands before the coming of white men. But we can be sure the cottonwood was chief among them, so prominent that to some homesick travelers it was symbolic of the lonely, forbidding Plains. In 1806 Lieutenant James Wilkinson was returning eastward along the Arkansas River after having left the Pike Expedition. Stopping near the site of modern Wichita, he gratefully noted in his journal: "I encamped on the bank of a large creek and discovered, for the first time, a species of wood differing from the cotton tree. I assure you the sight was more agreeable than a person would imagine; it was like meeting with an old acquaintance, from whom you had been separated a length of time; I even began to think myself approximating civilized settlements, although I was just entering on the hunting ground of the Osages."

The classic cottonwood of the tallgrass prairie and Mississippi Valley is *Populus deltoides,* the eastern cottonwood that extends from parts of the Atlantic seaboard as far west as the central Dakotas, Nebraska, Kansas, much of Oklahoma, and the eastern half of Texas. It takes its name from the strongly

triangular, delta-shaped leaf that is broader than long. Six other cottonwoods have similar leaves. There is the swamp cottonwood scattered through the East and South. Out in the shortgrass country, *deltoides* is replaced by the Plains cottonwood, *P. sargentii,* also called "sweet cottonwood" because of its milky juice. There is the Palmer cottonwood of west Texas, the Texas cottonwood in the northwestern part of the state, and the Rio Grande cottonwood—beloved tree of the New Mexican *bosques,* home of Bullock orioles and rookeries of Treganza blue herons. Finally, the Fremont cottonwood, my old friend of the desert camps and one of the fine trees of the Southwest. This is the cottonwood of the Grand Canyon's depths, the shade tree of Havasu Creek and the mouth of Canyon de Chelly, growing even out into deserty basins where trees of this size seem out of place.

Biggest of all is the black cottonwood that ranges along our Pacific Coast up through British Columbia and into the Yukon. Seldom more than 100 feet tall up in the foothills, it may tower 225 feet on a bole eight feet thick in parts of the Puget Sound Basin. But like the lance-leaf and narrowleaf cottonwoods, is it the real thing or just an outsized poplar putting on airs? To qualify as an honest-to-god cottonwood, some of us figure a tree ought to have that delta-shaped leaf. Otherwise, it must belong off with the willows, aspens, and other lesser members of the tribe.

Our common cottonwoods have all kinds of faults. They're messy. They grow unkempt in their old age. They tend to draw lightning. And in other ways, they don't fit in with the modern scheme of suburban living. The same things might be said of the old cottonwood breed of people—and wherever those trees and people have vanished, so has the West that stirred in both.

A few diehard leaves cling to the otherwise empty twigs of a Plains cottonwood. "The sweet inner bark of Plains cottonwood was relished by horses, and during George Custer's winter campaign of 1868–69 against Indians south of the Arkansas River, the mounts and pack animals were often fed cottonwood bark."

A PROPHECY
OF RESURRECTION

PHOTOGRAPHY BY ROBERT P. CARR

It seems as though the flowers of the witch-hazel were fairly entitled to the "booby-prize" of the vegetable world. Surely no other blossoms make their first appearance so invariably late upon the scene of action. The fringed gentian often begins to open its "meek and quiet eye" quite early in September. Certain species of goldenrod and aster continue to flower till late in the year, but they began putting forth their bright clusters before the summer was fairly over; while the elusively fragrant, pale yellow blossoms of the witch-hazel need hardly be expected till well on in October, when its leaves have fluttered earthward and its fruit has ripened. Does the pleasure which we experience at the spring-like apparition of this leafless yellow-flowered shrub in the autumn woods arise from the same depraved taste which is gratified by strawberries at Christmas, I wonder? Or is it that in the midst of death we have a foretaste of life; a prophecy of the great yearly resurrection which even now we may anticipate? (Mrs. William Starr Dana, from *How to Know the Wildflowers*, 1893.)

NUTS

TEXT BY HAL BORLAND · PHOTOGRAPHY BY LES LINE

The pecan is not native to New England. The closest it comes is Ohio. But it gets space here because it is an especially good nut tree—both Jefferson and Washington planted and grew magnificent pecan trees in Virginia—and because it illustrates a pioneer stupidity about natural resources that is almost incredible.

Pecan belongs to the walnut family. In Texas, one state to which it is native, it grows to tremendous size, sometimes a hundred and twenty feet high with a trunk thirty feet around. Its enormous limbs may spread its crown to a diameter of a hundred feet. The thin-shelled nuts, in their oval green husks, are one of the major nut crops of America. Well before settlers crossed the Alleghenies, traders and trappers brought pecan nuts to the coastal settlements, and plantation owners planted them. Thus grew many pecan groves from Virginia southward.

For many years only wild pecans came to market. The method of harvesting those wild ones now seems unbelievable. Nut-gatherers went through the woods, chose the largest, heaviest-bearing pecan trees, and when the nuts were ripe they cut down the trees. Then they put boys to work picking the nuts from the fallen giants. And that was the end of those pecan trees, forever. Next year they cut more trees to gather the nuts. Not until those magnificent pecan trees became scarce did they cease cutting them and begin planting and grafting new trees to replace the ones so stupidly destroyed. Today pecan trees are planted and grown in orchards like oranges.

Unlike most other members of the walnut family, the pecan is not particularly valued for its lumber. The nuts are its primary asset.

The shagbark, or shellbark as it is sometimes called, is the classic American hickory, probably the toughest tree on the continent. Weight for weight our hickory is stronger than steel, more elastic, and less heat-conductive. As fuel, it outranks coal, with more heat in it, pound for pound, than anthracite. Besides, the shagbarks have some of the sweetest nuts that grow in the woodland. What more can you ask of a tree?

The shagbark gets its name honestly. A mature tree has smoke-gray bark that is for-

Opposite page: nuts of pecan (Carya illinoensis). *Below: nuts of shagbark hickory* (Carya ovata).

ever separating into large plates, sometimes six inches wide and a foot and a half long, that curl away from the trunk at both ends. This gives a shaggy look to the tree, visible as far as you can see the tree itself, shaggy as a bear. This shagginess may start in fairly young trees, and at the base of old hickories there may be a whole pile of these bark plates, torn loose by the weather.

I marvel at the way a shagbark, or any hickory for that matter, opens its buds in the spring. Those big terminal buds are fat as a man's thumb. Their time approaches and they begin to twist, half open though with their tips still closed. Finally they twist themselves loose, and the whole bud and its contents are in sight, a yellow-green sheath tinged with red, and emerging from it the whole cluster of new leaves, tightly curled, and the catkins inside the leaves. It is like a miracle. No human hands ever packed half so much into so small a space.

Pioneers made boxes of hickory bark. They made ramrods for their guns from hickory wood; they made rungs for their chairs from it. They also made hoops for their barrels from hickory, hinges for their cabin doors, and handles for their axes.

Black walnut trees are rare in my corner of the country. In one little area near where I live they once grew as readily as willows, but elsewhere in New England the butternuts and the hickories dominated. Most of the walnuts around here were cut for gunstocks in the two World Wars. Those now left are mostly stragglers and cripples.

When it was reported that thieves had stolen the trunk of a black walnut tree from a cow pasture not fifty miles from here, it seemed incredible. But a little figuring showed why they took that tree and left the cows untouched. Peeled for surfacing on fancy plywood, that black walnut log would be worth more than fifteen thousand dollars.

The black walnut is not really beautiful. It has a sturdy central stalk or trunk, but it tends to be a broad tree, without grace. Its leaves are long and have fifteen or more leaflets opposite each other. Its fruits are black, rough-coated nuts enclosed in thick, yellowish-green husks rich in a very dark-brown dye. The meat of the nuts is rich, oily, and distinctly flavored. The outer hulls were used by pioneers as dyestuff for wool used to knit stockings. Anyone who picks or hulls walnuts has dark-dyed hands that do not bleach back to normal color for weeks.

Squirrels gather and hoard black walnuts. And they probably know more about nuts than we do. Some years ago a man who wanted walnut seedlings planted a hundred nuts in a row four inches deep. A few days later he found that squirrels had dug up ninety-two of those nuts. The other eight were right where they had been planted. The man dug them up, cracked them open, and found that none had a live kernel in it. The squirrels apparently knew that without even digging them up.

The hazelnut, also called filbert, is a shrub sometimes eight feet high, common in fencerows and thickety growth at the edge of

Opposite page: black walnut (Juglans nigra). *Below: nuts of American hazel* (Corylus americana).

timber patches. Its leaves are narrowly pointed or heart-shaped, rough above, pale below, three to five inches long. The staminate catkins are three to four inches long and bloom in April, when the early bees welcome them and spend long hours gathering their pollen. The fruit is a small, chestnut-brown nut, almost perfectly spherical, enclosed in a pair of broad, leafy, toothed bracts with many bristles at the base. The nutmeat is sweet and furnishes most of the hazelnuts on the market. They ripen in September.

A similar shrub, the beaked hazelnut, grows in hedgerows and thickets over much of the same area as the above species and also farther north. In virtually all details the two shrubs are the same, but the beaked hazelnuts are enclosed in a husk that terminates in a long, tubular beak.

We have a number of hazelnut bushes in our fencerows, and for years I planned to gather enough nuts to have occasional winter evenings of nut feasts, with hazelnuts, hickory nuts, and butternuts or black walnuts. But never yet have I been able to gather more than a scant handful of hazelnuts. The squirrels always beat me to them. I have tried picking them early, but they have no substance then. I have tried covering them with cheesecloth, but the squirrels go right through or under. I shall have to admire the bushes, envy the squirrels, and buy my hazelnuts at the market.

The butternut is New England's black walnut. It grows in the Midwest, too, out as far as Nebraska; but it is traditional in New England. As a tree, it is smaller than the black walnut, more branched, and more scraggly. Its leaves are compound, just like those of the black walnut, but they have longer stems and fewer leaflets, so the trees look sparsely leafed.

The nuts of the butternut are long and oval, but otherwise much like those of the black walnut, with that outer green husk, the black inner hull deeply corrugated, the sweet nutmeat sectioned in this tough, hard-to-crack hull. The shell or husk of the butternut has bristly little hairs that are full of a dark-brown dye, but the inside of that husk has a yellowish-orange dye. The squirrels in our woods love butternuts and leave middens of shell fragments at the base of the trees.

The meat of the butternut is flavored much like that of the black walnut, but it is more oily and it tends to go rancid. Indians and pioneers made oil from the butternuts and used it on their hair. Not many people seem to know how, but butternut sap makes good sugar, just like maple sap. It takes about four times as much sap from the butternut tree, however, as it does from a sugar maple to make a quart of syrup.

Butternut wood is relatively light in weight and easily worked. It is soft-textured and has a satiny finish. It was used in building fine carriages and is still used for interior finish in houses, where it does not warp or crack and seems to mellow with age. Many fine old American church altars were made of carved butternut wood.

Opposite page: butternut (Juglans cinerea).

VII
SPECIAL PLACES

IN THE NARROWS

TEXT BY LES LINE • PHOTOGRAPHY BY BILL RATCLIFFE

A gifted photographer lugs heavy camera gear through treacherous canyon bottom.

"The Zion Narrows is an arduous, twelve-mile hike and should not be taken lightly," warns the National Park Service bulletin. "It should never be attempted alone. There is no 'trail.' You will be wading in cold water, in the shade, crossing back and forth over slippery, algae-covered rocks. In the spring and early summer, the water is cold and swift and can be over your head in places. Hypothermia can be a real danger. Weather is unpredictable, and a sudden thunderstorm could cause the river to become a raging torrent. Escape areas are few and far between. Rescue by helicopter is impossible!"

The North Fork of the Virgin River, in Utah's Zion National Park, has been described as a "Jekyll-and-Hyde stream." Normally shallow and placid, mirroring colorful sandstone walls in its pools, the river can be transformed in brief minutes into a savage flood by a storm in the high country. The water has been known to rise 25 feet in a quarter-hour, carrying cottonwoods and boulders like mere twigs and pebbles in its roaring red surge.

Falling as rapidly as 90 feet in a mile, the Virgin River has excavated its course out of the heart of the Markagunt Plateau. Indeed, the excavation continues. The Virgin has been likened to an endless belt of sandpaper, carrying away three million tons of debris from the parklands each year. The spectacular geologic features of Zion are sculpted from Navajo sandstone—the remains of a great ancient desert. But the gorge of Zion Canyon was created when the river reached soft underlying shale beds of the Kayenta formation. Towering walls of sandstone were undermined when the stream eroded the weaker rock, causing huge slabs to collapse. The widening of the canyon was abetted, of course, by wind, rain, and frost.

Above the Temple of Sinawava, however, the Virgin River has yet to reach the soft shale. Here begins the Zion Narrows, where perpendicular walls loom 1,500 feet above the streambed. Where two men standing abreast can touch both sides of the chasm with their outstretched arms. Where, on September 17, 1961, a party of 26 hikers was caught by a flash flood—and five perished. Two of the bodies never were found.

"The flood began as a trickle, first over our shoe tops," one of the survivors related. "Then came what appeared to be a great wave of hay. It was pine needles. Then came the roar and finally, the trees and brush and boulders. It all happened almost within seconds."

Thus it was with some trepidation that Utah photographer Bill Ratcliffe entered the Narrows with the battered old view camera that has taken so many magnificent pictures of the Southwest's wonderlands. It was a strenuous, two-day trek that, as his notes on the following pages indicate, was not without moments of stress and danger. "Frankly, it was a great joy to see a trail at the end of the Narrows. But the memory of glowing reflections from multicolored canyon walls beckons me back. With just a 35mm camera and a little food."

*"I knew the trip would not be easy, but it was the most diffi-
cult—in physical stress—of my life. My companions were
Frank Hirst and his son. Frank commented several times on
how rough-going it was. There had been a lot of snow the
previous winter, and even in July the river was higher than
normal. Waist-deep water covered many places where
normally there would have been dry ground. The current was
swift, and we had to cross and recross the river hundreds of
times. I was loaded down with a large view camera and
tripod, film-holders, spare ground glass, light meter, food,
and sleeping bag. I covered my camera with a plastic bag in
case I slipped in midstream or stepped into a hole and had to
swim. At the Falls (page 138), formed by a logjam from flash
floods, we shed our clothes and swam in a deep pool. My
picture is softened by mist accumulating on the lens."*

"When I saw these stonefly exoskeletons on a wall covered with moss and liverworts, I had just one sheet of unexposed film loaded in a 4 × 5 holder. It was only two hours until darkness, and we were in the narrowest section where the river runs wall to wall and is about twelve feet wide. So I had no time to dig into my pack for fresh film, empty exposed holders and reload them, and take several shots. The light was poor: My exposure was seven seconds at f:8.

"I had told my friends to continue downstream. But I made the mistake of not watching their route through a deep pool. As I started out I found the water nearly to my shoulders. I held the camera high, but my pack was almost submerged. My real concern was that I could step into a hole and be in serious trouble—alone. Fortunately the water soon became waist-deep, and within ten minutes I caught up with my companions."

Above: "At Big Spring I found this lavish 'greenhouse' of ferns and monkey flowers growing for a hundred feet up the hillside. This was our first good source of drinking water, and we filled our canteens. I also took a bath with my camera. I was coming down from photographing the monkey flowers when I slipped on wet rocks—and landed in the river. My wide-angle lens was on the camera body, and the elements fogged up. I took the lens apart and tried to dry it off, but the shutter soon froze up." Right: "The hike through the narrowest section took eighteen hours. The water often was over my waist, and at least twice I had to remove my light meter from my shirt pocket to keep it dry. We were happy to finally reach the junction of Orderville Canyon, because it meant that the paved trail from the parking lot at the Temple of Sinawava was only an hour or so away."

TIGER IN THE ROAD!

TEXT BY GEOFFREY C. WARD • PHOTOGRAPHY BY GUNTER ZIESLER

The dust is the same as it was thirty years ago on the old Jaipur road that leads from Delhi to the Indian desert state of Rajasthan. It hangs in the hot still air above the field where a farmer and his haggard bullock scratch at the flat, beaten earth; swirls up from the sharp hooves of a herd of goats nibbling their way along the roadside; filters, gritty, between a traveler's teeth. But much else has changed since, as a boy, I last drove along this road to hunt.

Indian wildlife had seemed inexhaustible then. "Game" was all we ever called it. Partridges and peacocks bustled along the shoulders of the road back then, and the bright-green plots of wheat and mustard were home to blackbuck antelope, so many and so buoyantly curious that, at the sight of our Jeep rolling along a track then still traveled mostly by bullock carts, they sometimes left off their grazing to race in front of us, scores of them leaping over the road until the dust they kicked up made it impossible to see.

Now, blaring, overloaded trucks fill that same road, day and night, and the great bounding herds are gone. I wondered as the familiar landscape flashed by, what remained of the animals I had once pursued here with such heedless enthusiasm.

I: GAME

The Sariska Tiger Reserve where I was headed and where I had often hunted three decades ago was still a *game* sanctuary in those days; until very recently it had been the exclusive hunting reserve of the maharajas of Alwar, rulers of one of hundreds of small princely states and best remembered for the lavish tiger hunts they once organized for visitors from abroad.

In 1954, when my family and I arrived in India, where my father was to serve as consultant to a large foundation, I was just fourteen. I had not much wanted to come. City-bred and slowed down by polio that had been contracted two years earlier, I thought India simply sounded strange and impossibly far from my friends. But on the long shipboard journey I discovered *Jungle Lore* and several other books by Colonel Jim Corbett, the intrepid British dispatcher of man-eaters. His accounts of growing up in the Indian

forests were irresistible, and I secretly resolved that I would somehow experience as much of it as I could myself.

Perhaps my resolve was not so secret, for shortly after we moved into our house on what were then the outskirts of New Delhi, my father gave me a pellet gun. I began to prowl our compound and the scrub jungle that surrounded it, shooting at the doves that settled on the telephone wires and the little gray lizards that skittered along the red-brick garden wall. It was not the killing itself that drew me—though I can't deny that I enjoyed it—so much as the excitement of seeing how close I could get, and the extraordinary sense of power that shooting then represented. It was an activity well outside the tranquil world in which my parents had sought to raise my brother and sister and me, and perhaps more important, it provided me with vivid proof that even after polio I could affect things directly—even brutally—on my own.

In any case, two of my father's American friends took me on my first real hunt just a few miles outside the city one Sunday morning. They were after antelope. None were to be seen that day, but they lent me an old over-and-under, a combination .22 rifle and .410 shotgun, with which to shoot at anything else that turned up as we drove. I shot a fox, a rabbit, an owl, and a lynx with tufted

"I don't remember my mother's reaction—I suspect she was appalled—but my father seemed delighted. 'The boy is a crack shot,' he wrote home to my grandparents."

ears, then took the whole furry haul home and had myself photographed with it spread out around me on the lawn.

I don't remember my mother's reaction—I suspect she was appalled—but my father seemed delighted. "The boy is a crack shot," he wrote home to my grandparents. "Who would have thought it?" And he paid to have the owl and the lynx stuffed by a local taxidermist; the cat's snarling head hung in my upstairs bedroom for years, dust settling on its bright-pink tongue.

My parents bought the over-and-under for me, and when it proved too light and too slow to reload, they gave me a fine old Belgian twelve-gauge shotgun, purchased from two white-bearded Sikhs, proprietors of a gun shop in Connaught Circus that had served the shikar needs of several generations of British sahibs. I loved to visit their shop,

I studied up on wing shooting, doing my best to memorize how-to photo sequences featuring elderly Britons in plaid knickers, then stood in the garden taking pantomime aim at the taunting crows that flapped in and out of our trees.

Despite all my earnest backyard practice, I was never any good at shooting birds. I spent a number of frosty mornings crouched in blinds built in the midst of flooded fields, banging away without success at the ducks and geese that muttered overhead. A slender boy of twelve or so watched me most of one especially discouraging morning, drawn by all the noise my friends and I were making and by the rare spectacle of seeing a wet foreigner so near his home.

"What are you doing, sahib?" he finally asked after the last birds had moved too far off for us to scare into taking off again. "Do you want ducks? *I* will get them for you. Five rupees." How many did we want?

"Five," I said for no special reason; one number seemed as unlikely as another.

"Wait here," he said. The boy slipped into the water, which just covered his shoulders, and began walking slowly toward the sitting birds. Big clay water pots bobbed here and there, trapped in the fields when the rains came. He paused to break the neck off one of these, placed its round bottom over his head with just room enough to see, and resumed his slow, steady progress toward the ducks. It took him almost half an hour to reach them. But then, one by one and with only the slightest disturbance of the surface, he yanked five birds under, holding each there by its feet until it had stopped struggling. The hardest part was bringing them back; his thin legs trembled when he emerged, grinning, from the water, and it took both hands to carry his limp burden. We paid him double what he'd asked. I think that may have been my first faint inkling that there was something inherently foolish about shooting.

The four friends who watched with me as the boy drowned ducks that morning were my hunting companions throughout my three and a half years in India. All were much older than I. Bhagat and Harbans Singh were Sikh brothers, descended from a family of hunters, and fine shots. R. V. Raman was an airline executive for whom Bhagat Singh worked; he was an able, fast-talking, self-made man who seemed to have a hospitable friend or grateful client living near every likely forest and fishing stream in northern India. The last was my family's Christian driver, Mathew. (Those are not their real

partly just to admire the polished weapons and boxes of bright-red shotgun shells ranked in glass cases around its walls, but also because of the grave courtesy with which its owners pretended that this fourteen-year-old with round glasses was to be treated—as a mighty hunter.

No gun was ever better cared for than mine: its walnut stock always slippery with oil, its twin barrels gleaming, inside and out.

"To teach his son how to bag bigger game on the run, the maharaja ordered a railroad track built especially for him up one of the slopes in his state forest and had a flatcar fitted out with stuffed animals—tigers, leopards, an assortment of glass-eyed deer."

names; since these old friends are still living, and I am unclear about the Indian statute of limitations, I have thought it wise to invent new ones.) I suspect that these grown-ups were initially willing to take me hunting mostly because I had access to a Jeep, then still a relatively rare thing in India. But after a time they seemed to take a genuinely avuncular interest in my having as good a time as they did.

One of Raman's many friends was Vikram Singh, the Rao Raja of Alwar, and it was with him that we first hunted in the Sariska forest. He was a chunky little man, soft-spoken and round-faced and almost perpetually melancholy. He was the illegitimate son of the late maharaja—his title, Rao Raja, was itself a courtly euphemism for "bastard"—and there was a good deal of hard feeling between him and the half-brother then on the throne.

Because the boy could never rule, his father had decided when his son was still an infant that something else must be found for him to do with his time. Hunting was the answer, and although the Rao Raja grew wonderfully good at it, I don't think he ever liked it much. From early boyhood on he had been made to stand hip-deep in a nearby lake for hours at a time, firing at wildfowl. When the surface of the lake was at last empty, the birds driven elsewhere, he was still expected to continue shooting—hundreds, sometimes thousands of shells a day—until his ears rang and his cheek and shoul-

A sambar doe, munching aquatic plants while a cattle egret perches on its back, keeps a nervous eye out for the tigers which regularly chase down deer in the shallow marshland. The carcass will be carried to dense cover, where the tiger begins its feast at the choicest part of the deer, the rump.

der were blackened. To teach his son how to bag bigger game on the run, the maharaja ordered a railroad track built especially for him up one of the slopes in his state forest and had a flatcar fitted out with stuffed animals—tigers, leopards, an assortment of glass-eyed deer. A bullet-proof cab was constructed for the steam engine that pulled it so that the fireman and engineer could tow the targets up and down the hillside in relative safety. The young Rao Raja fired from a rocky perch across the valley, and when he had riddled all the beasts so that they sagged and spilled out most of their stuffing, replacements were nailed to the flatcar floor and the oversized shooting gallery hauled up the slope again.

The Rao Raja became a superb marksman. Without seeming even to aim he could plink copper anna pieces from the sky with a .22 rifle, and by the time I knew him in his mid-thirties, he had accounted for scores of tigers and leopards, hundreds of deer, thousands of birds from his family's preserve. His bravery was celebrated, too: Villagers like to tell of the time he entered a cave alone to track a wounded panther.

It had all bored him. "Too easy," he told me once. "Just bang, bang, bang." Still, he seemed to enjoy driving us into the forest. As he inched the Jeep through the bazaars of his battered old city or slowed to weave his way through one of the many villages that had once belonged to his father, it was clear that some things had not changed since the old days. Aged men called out greetings to the prince, bowing almost to the ground; at intersections they reached out to touch his feet. Women smiled shyly from behind the corners of their saris. Naked children waved. The Rao Raja acknowledged their greetings by lifting one hand slightly from the wheel. At first all this obeisance seemed disturbing,

but before long I was doing my best to mimic his princely nonchalance.

In British times, only members of the royal family had been permitted to shoot at Sariska; the muzzle of anyone else's weapon carried through their land was sealed with wax. By the time I first saw it, the forest was at least officially off limits even to the Rao Raja—though neither he nor the forest officers in charge seemed willing to admit it. He did not so much as slow the Jeep at the gatehouse, and the game wardens in khaki all saluted as we roared past.

The Rao Raja knew every parched hillside and stony ravine.

"Now," he said, slowing the Jeep as we approached a forest curve one afternoon. "Around the corner, in the clearing on your left, you will find seven partridge." We stopped. "Get out, shoot just one, then come right back." I got down and walked up the road, aware that he was watching, knowing I was supposed to hold up my end, but knowing also that no one, not even the Rao Raja of Alwar, could possibly know how many birds there would be in an unseen clearing. I saw nothing at first; the clearing seemed empty. But as I stared I began to see them; seven brown-gray birds almost invisible against the brown-gray earth.

I stamped my foot, and when the startled partridges whirred into the air I fired both barrels. Not a feather fell.

"Bad shooting," the prince said as we drove off again.

Most of our hunting at Sariska was done at night, however, and the Rao Raja usually found something else to do just as we were about to set out. I suspect he thought nightshooting unsporting but was too polite to say so to his guests. Instead, we were sometimes driven into the dark forest by a local friend of his, a raffish Parsi liquor distributor from Bombay, who owned a sprawling bungalow, a herd of polo ponies, and a bright-red roofless Buick built in the 1930s and equipped with twin spotlights powerful enough to transfix any animal we passed. (The car looked a good deal more impressive than it was: Late one afternoon, as we rolled down a steep road, I was startled to see something big and black bounding along ahead of us on the left; it was the rear wheel; seconds later we fetched up against the hillside and had to be towed back to town.) From that Buick's leather-covered back seat one night, I fired at a pair of anonymous eyes and killed a chousingha, or four-horned antelope, the smallest and rarest of all Indian antelope. Since this dainty animal was even then officially protected, I had to leave its small broken body

A black-naped hare: The shooting continued all through the night.

where it had fallen, for fear someone would turn us in.

Most of my contacts with the Sariska forest were like that—urgent, ignorant, aimed only at ending lives I did not remotely understand. One favorite road twisted up a stony hillside past several natural pools. A cold mist hung perpetually in this valley on winter nights, and whenever we drove through it we wrapped ourselves in blankets and put up the Jeep's windscreen to keep off the chill. A big sambar stag suddenly appeared on the right side of the road one night, his shaggy neck and impressive antlers hung with branches torn from the brush through which he had just come. We stopped. He began to step slowly across the road, head back, one rolling eye glittering in the headlights. I struggled to get to my feet, clawing at the blankets so that I could take aim over the windscreen. My shotgun caught. I fell back. Behind me my friends tried to hold me upright, whispering, "Shoot! Shoot!" Before I could, the stag disappeared down the hillside on our left. I dreamed of him for years.

Another night, not far from there, our spotlight picked out a whole constellation of gleaming eyes. Unable to tell stags from does—or even for sure what sort of animals these were—I jumped down to creep closer, careful to keep from being silhouetted in the paralyzing beam. My friends waited in the Jeep. I had moved twenty yards or so into the forest when I saw in the topmost branches of the trees the faint shifting glow that meant another car was coming. "Game wardens," I heard Raman say. "Come back!" Mathew called to me: "Hurry up. The patrol is coming." He started the motor. The lights were coming closer, the car's whine now unmistakable. Thorn bushes clawed at my legs. An unseen hole sent me sprawling. "Stay there," Mathew shouted. "We'll come back for you."

The Jeep sped away. Alone now in the black forest, I could hear the herd moving off through the thickets as the sound of the second car drew nearer. Its lights swung around a curve and the car slid to a stop perhaps twenty feet from where I lay on top of my shotgun; I was certain I was about to be seen, arrested, imprisoned. A spotlight's beam swung over my head, lighting up the thorn bush beneath which I was huddled. A gun barrel slid through the car's front window; two more muzzles appeared at the back. Not game wardens. Poachers. Now I would be shot. I held my breath.

"Nothing. I told you, *nothing*," a voice said from inside the car. "Why don't you listen to me?"

"I'm telling you, something moved in there. I saw it."

More lights appeared in the trees; another motor could be heard. The guns were withdrawn and the car pulled away, spattering me with gravel. I stayed where I was. Moments later my friends drove up. They had circled back for me, and it was their lights that had driven off the strangers.

We spent hour upon hour on those dark roads, peering along the spotlight's beam as it probed and poked its way between the trees and through the grass. Here and there it picked out a remnant of the sanctuary's royal past: gateposts carved with the Alwar coat of arms; stone shooting towers; the huge abandoned palace that had once served as the maharaja's hunting lodge, looming white above the undergrowth that choked its abandoned garden.

By three or four in the morning, when every stump in the forest seemed a crouching tiger to our exhausted eyes, we returned to the little Canal Department rest house where we stayed when we were not the Rao Raja's guests. There, the resident cook would prepare dinner for us—curried venison if we'd been lucky; chicken otherwise—while we sat on string beds around the fire, talking over the night's hunting. I rarely managed to stay awake long enough to eat, drifting off beneath the stars, surrounded by the fire's warmth and the smell of woodsmoke, listening to the distant gunfire that meant other poachers were still out on the road, and to the sleepy voices of my friends, chuckling at jokes in Hindi I only half-understood.

Sometimes the far-off shooting continued all night. It was echoing all over the subcontinent then. Understandably enough, free India's first priority was the growing of enough food to feed her restless, fast-growing population. In the face of that over-

A sloth bear: And the rulers were implausible conservationists.

whelming need, old forestry practices introduced by the British came to seem somehow undemocratic. Forests were systematically ravaged for timber and fuel, thrown open to grazers, leveled to provide farmers with more land. Gun licenses were issued wholesale for crop protection, an invitation to massive poaching; animals not shot were trapped or poisoned. The export of skins and hides became a major source of foreign exchange. Shikar outfitters brought in wealthy foreign sportsmen to mop up what the villagers had overlooked. Demoralized and underpaid officials could earn more by looking the other way than by enforcing wildlife statutes no one bothered about much anymore.

Forest cover shrank steadily; wildlife vanished. Even the once ubiquitous jackals, whose weird cackling yowls had kept us awake in New Delhi itself, were all but annihilated for their skins. The tiger provided the most dramatic evidence of what was happening everywhere. At the turn of the 20th Century, there were at least 40,000 tigers in India (some authorities put the figure at 50,000). By 1972 there were just over 1,800, concentrated largely in a few pockets of forest that had once been the exclusive preserves of the Indian princes.

These rulers were implausible conservationists. Their preserves were after all intended primarily to assure them of a steady supply of birds and animals at which to shoot. The sheer volume of game a prince could parade past his guests' guns provided vivid evidence of his wealth and hospitality.

The Maharaja of Bharatpur, a small state not far from Sariska, for example, was host to an annual wildlife shoot; on a single deafening morning in 1938, he and thirty-seven guests (including the British viceroy, Lord Linlithgow) accounted for 4,327 ducks and geese. Tigers were the top trophy, of course, and the princes vied with one another to see who could run up the highest tally; the hands-down winner was the last Maharaja of Surguja, who claimed 1,150. No other prince ever managed to overtake him—not even when some of the over-eager among them took to including in their lifetime totals every fetus found in pregnant tigresses.

Still, the royal preserves offered wildlife a kind of qualified but genuine sanctuary rarely found elsewhere. In the early 1970s, concerned citizens finally forced the Indian government to realize what it had allowed to happen, to ban shooting and the export of wild animal skins, and to launch Project Tiger as a last-minute effort to rescue the tiger and something of the complex ecosystem upon which it depended. Several of the nine sanctuaries it set aside were former royal preserves. Sariska was not initially one of them. Poaching continued there unabated until 1978, when it was at last added to the roster of tiger reserves that now numbers fifteen.

Since I knew it as a boy, the city of Alwar has become an industrial center, ringed with smokestacks. A billboard on the main road reads WELCOME TO KELVINATOR COUNTRY. Its feudal past has largely been forgotten,

At Ranthambhore National Park, a lakeshore pavilion and the battlements of a 10th-Century fortress on the hilltop.

though tourists sometimes visit the florid city palace and an old bronze cannon still guards a traffic island around which oblivious trucks and motor scooters now flow without a break. The Rao Raja died several years ago, a local man told me; during his last years he had been forced to take a relatively minor bureaucratic job with the democratic government he had despised.

But Sariska itself at first seemed unchanged. It remains a parched, inhospitable place, a cluster of sharp quartzite hills and valleys thinly covered with drab forest, relieved only here and there by bursts of brilliant green that signal the presence of a spring or streambed. There is very little rain, and most of what there is of it falls between July and September; much of the rest of the year the dry leaves of the dhok trees that cover all but the steepest slopes are more or less the same dispiriting color as the fine dust that is thrown into the air at the slightest movement of man or animal. Were the terrain more congenial, the Sariska forest would long ago have been cut and farmed and grazed into oblivion.

The old royal hunting lodge that had been deserted and overgrown in my day has recently been reopened as the Sariska Palace, a luxury hotel, and painted a gaudy yellow, blue, and pink. A bright banner flies again from the central flagstaff: green, red, black, and saffron stripes (Alwar's princely colors, the manager told me, "but rearranged, so no one will accuse us of monarchism"). Inside, the public rooms are oddly gloomy—huge, high-ceilinged, and lit by bare bulbs so feeble that I could see every detail of the glowing filaments. The green walls are hung with white skulls of deer. Tigers in glass cases crouch in the corners; the one next to my table in the dining room was undersized, its stripes faded to tan, its claws rotted away, its tail only recently reattached with plaster.

The lodge is a monument to the turn-of-the-century pretensions of Maharaja Jay Singh of Alwar, one of India's most bizarre and sinister princes. Jay Singh believed himself the earthly incarnation of the god Rama and was therefore especially rigorous in his orthodoxy: He wore black silk gloves even when shaking hands with the English king. He had two vast towered kitchens, three stories tall, built on either side of his hunting lodge, one for his own food, the other for the preparation of the unclean things his foreign guests insisted upon eating. And he was fiercely proud. Visiting the Rolls Royce showroom in London sometime during the 1920s, he asked how much a certain model cost. The salesman smiled; no Indian could possi-

bly afford such a vehicle, he said. Jay Singh ordered ten on the spot, had them shipped home and their roofs torn off; then, to the distress of the Rolls Royce company and the delight of his fellow princes, sent them out from his city palace each morning to collect his subjects' garbage.

He privately loathed the British, but always treated those Britons who visited his preserve with distant but elaborate courtesy. Goats were tied near the fountain in the center of the garden; the gate was left open so that leopards would get used to padding past the lawn furniture in search of easy meals. The after-dinner kills in the moonlit garden are said to have delighted the ladies seated on the veranda. His entire state army was routinely marshaled to beat the Sariska forests for his guests, squads of infantry and cavalry and an elephant corps driving before them everything that walked or flew. The shooting towers I had seen as a boy were his, too; tall, thick-walled, and provided with cushions and gun slits so that visitors could safely sit and sip their whiskey sodas while waiting for a tiger to kill the plaintive buffalo calf tethered to an iron ring just a few steps away.

When no visitors were about, Jay Singh's private life was filled with cruelty. It amused him to stake out elderly widows and small children as tiger bait. He was said to be given to sexual excesses with boys as well as with the young women his agents routinely kidnapped off the streets of his city. Evenings in his private chambers sometimes ended in murder. More than half his state's revenues went to pay for his personal extravagances. The British did nothing about any of this. Sir Edwin Montague, the Secretary of State for India, is said to have particularly admired Jay Singh's unfailing good manners. But in 1933 the maharaja went too far: After his polo pony threw him during a hotly contested game he doused it with gasoline and set it ablaze. At that, the animal-loving British exiled him forever from his state.

Under Project Tiger, access to Jay Singh's forests is now rigorously controlled. No visitor can enter the reserve on foot or without a forest guard to serve as guide. Mine was named Ramchandran Singh, a slender young man with a waxed moustache and white teeth. Beyond the gate, the scrub forest still spread out on either side of the narrow tarmac road that ran between the brown hills, just as I remembered. Within a hundred yards I spotted two nilgai moving through the roadside brush on our left. My friends and I had shot a good many of these big

A fig tree smothers the ruins of a maharaja's summer place.

157

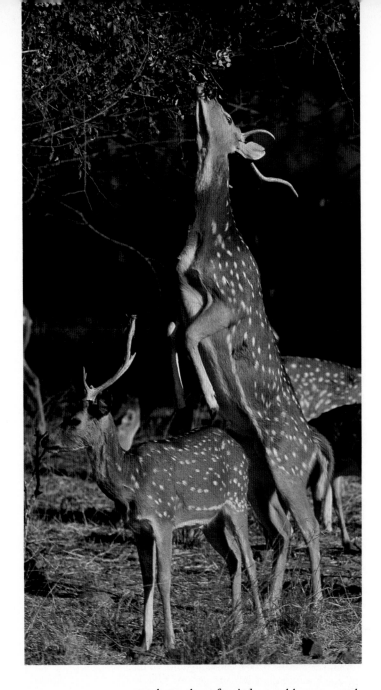

or another of the seven artificial waterholes that now line the road.

There were nilgai and sambar in groups of five and six. Chital, the red-dappled deer that must be among the most beautiful on Earth, could be seen in herds of ten to twenty. There had been no chital at all when I hunted at Sariska. Now they seemed to be everywhere—some 8,000 of them, if the official figures are correct—all descended from three or four terrified animals chased here by village dogs when a royal deer park nearby was obliterated not long after I left India in 1957. And I had never before seen sambar in the daytime; there are now 6,000 of them.

For someone who remembered this place as dark and mysterious, its animals as furtive, even ghostly, Sariska was now a revelation. It was the end of the mating season, Ramchandran told me. Chital fawns minced through the grass. A sambar stag, still larger than the one of which I sometimes still dreamed, lowered his great head and horns and sprayed himself spectacularly with urine. The smell, Ramchandran assured me, would make him irresistible to the does that waited a few yards away. Here and there among the trees, young chital stags clashed with elaborate ceremony. Heads down, antlers locked, feet braced, they strained back and forth, whining with the effort like big angry babies. Then they simultaneously lifted their heads, froze to glare into one another's eyes

antelope whose fancied resemblance to cattle makes some Hindus revere them as sacred; their meat was in fact a fair substitute for the beef which for obvious reasons was rarely available in India. They are ungainly, even ludicrous animals—the slate-gray males have white-striped ankles and a ragged goatee and are built on a sort of slant—but it was wonderful to see them again, and so close to the road. What good luck, I thought, and clapped Ramchandran on the shoulder.

He seemed a little startled at my enthusiasm. We would see many more, he assured me. I thought he was being overly optimistic. I knew this place, after all; one or two brief glimpses like this were all one could expect. But within half a mile or so, we were surrounded by hundreds of antelope and deer grazing in the feathery grass or filing to one from a distance of perhaps two feet, and went back at it.

It was almost too much. I had a sense after a while that I was in some sort of safari park, that the herds must be only half-wild. This feeling intensified when the animals did not even flinch as a brightly painted tour bus hurled past us, its passengers leaning out the windows to hoot at them.

An afternoon in a small cinder-block blind on the edge of a waterhole changed my mind. Lying on a mattress in the dark cool interior of the hide, just thirty feet from the farthest edge of the muddy pool, I found myself in the midst of a steady, slow-moving procession of thirsty animals whose every waking moment was obviously spent in terror— not of the people passing by in vehicles, who no longer represent a menace to them, but of the unseen tigers that can lie hidden anywhere. The deer and antelope approach the water with infinite wariness, nostrils flaring to catch the faintest scent, ears alert for telltale sounds, big eyes wide and staring, placing their hooves gingerly, as if they feared the earth itself might suddenly move beneath them.

The delicate four-horned antelope that drink near noon seemed most skittish. It took each one two or three tries to work up the courage to actually approach the pool; once each had swallowed its precious mouthful of water, it raced back to the woods in

frenzied bounds. But the larger animals were only slightly less tentative. Later that afternoon, ten chital were bunched along one side of the pool and a big sambar stag was approaching slowly, ready to join a pair of does already at the water. Suddenly two baby wild boar ran into the clearing, kicking up a tiny cloud of dust with their frantic trotters. The stag bellowed as if two tigers were charging and galloped toward the forest; his does beat him to the tree line. The chital had already vanished. With the big clearing to themselves, the piglets raced back and forth in perfect tandem for perhaps three minutes before rushing off again.

I witnessed more forest life in that single afternoon than I'd seen during three and a half years of hunting. A big nilgai stalked down to the water, the insides of his twitching ears glowing pink before he dipped his head. A chital stag slipped up behind him and, although there was plenty of room, jolted him hard in the backside with his antlers. The startled nilgai, far larger than his tormentor but equipped with horns no longer than my index finger, trotted heavily away. The deer's antlers reach extraordinary size now that hunting has been ended. One old chital, his blunt muzzle gray with age, bore horns so huge and heavy that it seemed miraculous he could hold them upright, let alone move through the forest without help.

The sounds of the forest were new to me, too. One after another all afternoon, the far-off chital stags challenged one another, their horny wheezes echoing from the slopes. When a herd of perhaps twenty nervous young chital shouldered their way to the edge of the pool, they kept up a high-pitched, running commentary of squeals and whines, as if to reassure one another that it was really all right to take a moment out from their eternal vigilance to drink. A few moments later, five peafowl waddled down to the water. While the hens drank, the lone male began his courting dance, his huge fan spread out above him. When that iridescent spectacle failed to impress one thirsty hen, he stood stock still behind her and began literally to vibrate with yearning, his clashing feathers producing an astonishingly loud chatter. It certainly impressed me, but the hen for which it was intended remained unmoved.

No tiger came to the pool while I was there. I had never seen one at Sariska in the old days, either. (Once I thought I had, at night; I took aim at its striped haunch, then held my fire, hoping the half-hidden animal would move and offer me a clearer shot. It did; it was a hyena.) After dark that first

159

evening, and for three evenings after that, Ramchandran tried very hard to show me a tiger. He drove with me up and down the dark roads I remembered so well, holding a spotlight out the window and swinging its white beam furiously from one side of the road to the other so as not to leave a yard of forest unexamined.

"Sambar," he would whisper, able instantly to see the whole outline of an animal whose gleaming eyes were all I had time to glimpse, then whirled to catch a chital as it faded into the brush on the opposite side. Several porcupines rattled across the road. A civet tumbled after one of them, a white ball in the headlights, its striped tail stretched out behind it.

But no tiger ever appeared. "One thing," Ramchandran muttered to the driver, "VIPs *never* see a tiger."

Before heading back to the hotel for the last time, we stopped at a guard post deep in the sanctuary. It was a cold night, and the five forest guards who lived there made room for us around their fire; one poured me a cup of spiced tea. I was sorry at having failed again to see a tiger where I had always hoped to see one. Perhaps I would do better at the Ranthambhore Tiger Reserve, the next stop on my trip. But as I sipped the tea, my disappointment was swept away by memory. Everything came back to me from thirty years before: the velvet black of the surrounding hills against the star-filled sky; the low voices of my companions; the smell and welcome warmth of the fire. There was no sound of distant shooting now; it had been replaced by a new and comforting sound: From just beyond the firelight came the strenuous

clacking of two chital stags, contesting to insure the future of their herd.

II: TIGERS

When I told Ramchandran that I was on my way to Ranthambhore with an introduction to its field director, Fateh Singh Rathore, he was clearly impressed. "A *very* dangerous man," he said, by which I think he meant that Fateh Singh was brave and resolute. He is in fact a legend among Indian conservationists. No wildlife official has worked harder or sacrificed more to protect the land and animals under his care; none has seen his hard work crowned with greater success. Under his implacable protection, the number of tigers flourishing at Ranthambhore has grown from fourteen to forty in just thirteen years. "You will see a tiger at Ranthambhore," Ramchandran assured me as I left Sariska. "Fateh Singh can *always* show you one."

Ranthambhore is no more lush than Sariska; neon parakeets and iridescent bee-eaters provide the brightest spots of green among its seared hillsides. But it is far more beautiful. The towers and sprawling battlements of an abandoned 10th Century fortress cover the top of its highest hill. For centuries, Ranthambhore was the hunting preserve of the princes of Jaipur. Scattered all through its forests are crumbling walls, fallen temples, and carved *chatris*—domed monuments, each marking the spot where some long forgotten man of consequence was cremated.

A chain of three small, bright-blue lakes runs down the center of the preserve, and I stayed for several days on the shore of the largest of these, in a restored pavilion called the Jogi Mahal. From its cool veranda I watched crocodiles and soft-shelled turtles sun themselves and herds of chital browse along the shore. Sambar came down to the water, too, and splashed right in to stay for hours, immersed among succulent lotus pads, their broad backs becoming islands for snowy egrets.

This extraordinary place is Fateh Singh's domain. He is a Rathore, a member of the ancient clan whose chief is the former Maharajah of Jodhpur. He has none of his ancestors' bloody-mindedness, but he has inherited their fascination with the forest and their sense of proprietorship over everything that lives within it. He speaks of Ranthambhore as "my park," its tigers as "my tigers."

Fateh Singh is forty-five years old, short, and chesty, with a steel-gray moustache. He is given to sporty hats, sunglasses, and dapper green safari clothes. There is little of the ascetic about him: He savors a bawdy joke and a stiff drink on the rooftop of his forest home after dark, and he lets nothing interfere with his favorite situation comedy in Hindi, which he watches on a small black-and-white set powered by a car battery.

But his animals come first, always. Even his marriage was allowed to founder on that premise.

"There's your music!" he shouted as we drank a cup of tea shortly after dawn on my first morning at Ranthambhore. We were listening to the steady *poot-poot-poot* of the coppersmith which, he said, meant that summer was coming fast. The forest chorus grew more complex. The shrill triple-noted call of the gray partridge blended discordantly with the contralto *peeoar* of the peacocks, the insistent *Did-you-do-it? Did-you-do-it?* of the lapwings, and finally, the deep

solemn hooting of the gray langur monkeys. "They're telling each other 'I'm okay, you're okay,'" Fateh said. "Glad they got through another night."

Suddenly, the langurs' mellow choruses turned to angry, hawking coughs. We put down our cups and raced for Fateh's Jeep. From their perches in the tops of trees, langurs are often the first to announce the presence of a prowling tiger. We would spend the next four days like firefighters, careening over the stony landscape to answer every alarm. As we drove, Fateh sat ramrod stiff in the back, humming to himself at the sheer pleasure of being in his forest and occasionally pointing out one or another of the 275 species of birds seen there.

The deer and antelope at Ranthambhore are no less serene in the presence of human beings in vehicles than they are at Sariska, but they are less thickly concentrated and are more often screened by the trees and grass

Opposite page: The jungle cat's legs are long for running down prey. Below: Langur monkeys are often the first to announce a prowling tiger.

and thorny undergrowth that now grows everywhere. Part of the reason that Sariska had seemed initially so like a zoo was that buffalo and cattle are still permitted to browse along its roadsides during the day, chewing away the foliage and opening up broad, artificial vistas. Local politics has prevented Sariska's field director from pressing forward with plans to shift several cattle camps out of the reserve. There had always been a certain tension between the Sariska herdsmen and the forests their voracious animals steadily devoured. One night thirty years ago, we encountered a very old man walking all alone along a dark forest road, his only weapon the long-handled ax with which he cut fodder from the trees when his buffalo had eaten everything else within reach. What was he doing there at such an hour? we asked. "Sahib, last week I owned two buffalo," he said. "A tiger has killed one. Now I will kill the tiger before he can get the other one." We took him home to his village. Such people are not easily persuaded to change their ways and so far, in Sariska at least, it has been thought best to leave the squatters alone.

At Ranthambhore, however, Fateh Singh had felt differently. There had been sixteen villages in his preserve, a thousand villagers, perhaps 10,000 head of livestock. The life they led there was meager and marginal—their herds were scrawny; the land they farmed was stony and exhausted—but for more than two centuries it was all their ancestors had known and no one had wanted to leave. Fateh Singh could have resorted to

force. (When herdsmen were barred from the Kaladeo Bird Sanctuary that now occupies the broad artificial lake where the maharajas of Bharatpur once organized their annual slaughter of wildfowl, there was an angry confrontation with the local police that left five villagers dead and thirty-five more wounded.) Instead, he used patience and persuasion, concentrating on the younger and better-educated headmen. He was authorized to offer them additional land, if they agreed to move to a new site twenty kilometers outside the sanctuary on far better land than they had ever known. Two new temples would be built there for each old one left behind. There would be a new school, access to a post office, improved breeding stock, a modern well and electricity with which to pump its precious water. If they were wary of government promises, he told them, they should hold him personally responsible for making good on all of them. Like his princely ancestors he would provide for them.

But mixed in with these material incentives was a spiritual message as well. The forest and all its creatures were the creation of the gods, he argued over the village fires: Did not the great goddess Durga herself ride a tiger? No man had a right to disturb that divine creation; the forests must be left to grow back, to become again what their creator had intended. To continue to live in the forest was to commit a kind of blasphemy.

When the day finally came and trucks drew up to carry the villagers' few belongings to their new homes, many of them wept. One old man hugged a gnarled tree, crying that his father and grandfather had rested in its shade, that such fine shade could never be obtained elsewhere. Fateh Singh cried with them. But he made sure they went.

The lands their herds had ravaged are thickly overgrown now, but some of their crumbling huts still stand, and one day not long ago, Fateh Singh took the headman of one of the old villages back to see its transformed site. A tiger lay sleeping in one of the ruined houses. The headman was delighted. "Now we are happy," he said. "The goddess has come."

Despite Ramchandran's confidence in him and Fateh Singh's intimate knowledge of the Ranthambhore tigers (half of which he knows by name and can identify at a glance), even he cannot summon up a tiger at will to show to visitors. We drove through his preserve for four days, off and on, listening for the alarm calls of deer and monkeys and leaning down from time to time to examine the pug marks of tigers that seemed always to have just preceded us on the twisting forest track.

In the late afternoons we parked overlooking one or another of the lakes, hoping to see a tiger charge out of the grass to kill one of the hundreds of deer feeding there. One evening as we sat watching in the fading golden light we spotted two figures strolling along the path toward us, a tall Englishman hung with binoculars and wearing khaki shorts, arm in arm with an eighty-year-old Dutch woman whom I recognized as a fellow guest at the Jogi Mahal. The two had dawdled along obliviously for hundreds of yards between high yellow walls of dhok grass whose soft sibilance in even a faint breeze can disguise the movements of the clumsiest tiger. Fateh was apoplectic. "Stupid! Stupid! Bloody idiots!" he shouted at the startled visitors, pulling them into his Jeep. "I should throw you out of this park. You will get my tigers killed."

People, not animals, remain his most vexing problem. In the heart of the Ranthambhore fortress is a temple dedicated to Ganesa, the fat, amiable, elephant-headed god who blesses all new ventures, including marriage and childbearing. Small groups of worshippers seeking his favor climb the hill every morning, and on one annual festival day some 10,000 pilgrims troop along the main sanctuary road to converge on the temple. Even Fateh Singh does not dare interfere with the rights of the faithful to worship where they please, but he does worry about what might happen if one of his tigers should someday attack a pilgrim. Then, too, scattered among the deepest ravines, live a handful of solitary sadhus. These ascetic hermits have vowed to end their days there, praying in the wilderness. Fateh isn't sure how many there are—perhaps five, he says—and so far, the animals have left them alone. The sadhus attribute this to the power of their belief; Fateh credits "damned good luck."

Fateh does the best he can to control the rest of those who seek admission to his sanctuary. No one is allowed to walk in the forest. Tourists must be driven by trained guards, and a good deal of his time is spent allocating seats for them among the small fleet of spavined vehicles at his disposal. One evening I counted thirty-one spectators packed into five parked Jeeps, all of us watching to see if a single, noisy sambar calf would find its missing mother before a hungry predator found it. (It did.)

The most serious trouble still comes from local people. A dozen villages have been successfully shifted out of the park, but thirty more ring its perimeter. The trees have always provided fuel for their cook fires; its grass and undergrowth have fed their herds. The villagers are only bewildered and angered by the notion that their ancient forest should suddenly be off limits to them. Women slip into the park through hidden ravines to cut grass, carrying out great heaps of it on their heads. Troops of woodcutters enter, too, and so do herdsmen with their grazing animals and tribal hunters with packs of trained dogs.

Fateh Singh and his forest guards do their best to fend them all off, but it is not easy. He has too few men to patrol the entire border of the park. The grass-cutters hide their curved blades beneath their skirts, then charge the guards with molestation when they are searched. When disputes arise, local politicians often favor the villagers—who can vote—over animals that cannot. Three years ago, Fateh Singh himself was set upon by some fifty angry herdsmen. They beat him unconscious, broke his arm, shattered his kneecap, and left him for dead. (He spent three months in a hospital, then was awarded India's highest civilian medal for valor.)

One morning during my visit, a forest guard staggered into the field director's office, the side of his face bruised and badly swollen. He had been beaten by four woodcutters. Fateh Singh instantly dispatched a party of his own men to retaliate in kind. "We can't treat these people the way you do in America," he said. "No psychiatrists here. We don't ask, '*Why* do you do this?' We just give them a good bashing."

He is a stern sovereign, but he tries hard to

On opposite page are nilgai: "I witnessed more life in a single afternoon that I'd seen during three and a half years of hunting." Below: Fateh Singh Rathore feeds langur monkeys.

TEJBIR SINGH

be fair. When, not long ago, the former Maharani of Jaipur visited her family's old hunting lodge just outside the park and ordered that several partridges be shot for her guests' luncheon, Fateh Singh took her to court. "There must be the same law for rich and for poor," he told me. The Maharani's case is just one of some three hundred he still has pending in the Indian courts.

His is an intensely personal struggle. Here and there across India other determined individuals have also managed to save patches of forest and the wildlife that lives within them, at least for the moment. But their achievements, like Fateh Singh's, will remain fragile, tenuous, until the ordinary people who live nearby come to see their value. So far they do not. Whenever Fateh leaves his stronghold, even for a few days, interlopers stream across its borders and have to be driven out again when he gets back. "It's an endless war," he told me as we drove through the forest on my last morning at Ranthambhore, and it is one he would prefer not to have to fight. Despite almost daily threats and his own near-fatal beating, he refuses to carry a gun and won't let his men carry them either. "I'm too hot-tempered," he told me. "If I had a gun I know I would shoot someone."

"We want to be friendly," he said, "to work *with* the people, not against them. What we need is a 'Project People for Project Tiger.'" He has called for teams of conservation workers to move from village to village, explaining the long-term benefits of keeping the forests intact; a program to recruit tribal hunters into the forest service so that their forest skills can be used to save animals rather than slaughter them. The periphery of the park should be replanted with improved grasses for harvesting, he says, but only to nourish stall-fed livestock—and funds must be found to encourage traditional herdsmen to abandon their inferior wasteful animals in favor of improved breeds. All of this will take time and money and coordinated planning.

In the meantime, the tigers of Ranthambhore have only Fateh Singh. He has worked within the sanctuary for twenty of his twenty-five years in the forest service, and his success has several times led his superiors at Delhi to try to promote him to a desk job. He always turns them down because he plans to stay in one place—and in charge—until he retires. "I know this place," he explained, rising in his seat to peer over the tops of the thorn bushes. "I'm not happy anywhere else. I've bought myself a farm at the edge of the forest so that every day until I die I can

drive over and visit my park."

He clutched my shoulder. "Tiger in the road," he said. Perhaps forty feet ahead of us a tiger sat in the middle of the track. It filled the track, in fact, and seemed somehow to fill the forest that stretched away on either side as well. Nothing had prepared me for its size or for the palpable sense of menace and power that emanated from it. "His name is Akbar," Fateh whispered, beginning softly to hum with pleasure at the sight of him. "About five hundred pounds."

The tiger rose slowly to his feet. Everything about him seemed outsized: his big round ruffed face; his massive shoulders and blazing coat; his empty belly that hung in

folds and had finally forced him into the open to hunt; his long twitching tail. It seemed inconceivable that such a big, vivid animal could have stayed hidden in this drab open forest for so long.

We sat very still in the open Jeep as the tiger stared at us. "He's a good boy," Fateh said, still humming. I devoutly hoped so. The tiger turned and cocked his huge head to listen as a sambar called from a clearing off to our left; then, after fixing us with one more steady glance, he slipped silently into the grass. Neither his smiling protector nor his protector's wary guest had been worth so much as a growl.

III: BLACKBUCK

I had only dreamed of tigers as a boy. What I really hunted were blackbuck, fleet delicate antelope whose spiraling horns and richly patterned skins made handsome trophies. They had been scattered nearly everywhere across the northern Indian plains then, and my friends and I had traveled nearly everywhere in search of them.

I knew them then only as targets, of course. Sometimes Bhagat Singh shot them with his old rifle from what always seemed to me to be fantastic distances. Much more often, we pursued them in our Jeep, Mathew at

the wheel, careening around thorn bushes at forty miles an hour, slamming across rutted fields, flying over the tamped mud walls that separated one man's crop from the next, while my friends and I struggled both to stay in our seats and to fire buckshot into the frantic animals zigzagging ahead of us. Once, our Jeep turned entirely over, though with such merciful slowness that we were all able to step safely out into the soft dust. An amused old farmer and his bullocks came along and helped us right ourselves. At harvest time we had to be particularly careful not to hit the village women who were hidden, kneeling, in the billowing wheat.

I must have shot thirty blackbuck during my years in India. At the end of one especially busy day my friends and I drove home with thirteen of them heaped beneath a flapping tarpaulin in the back of our Jeep, enough to fill our freezer and those of our friends for several months. I could sense always that my parents were of two minds about my shooting. They liked having the fresh meat (a rare thing then in Delhi), and they thought it good that I had a hobby that got me out of the house and into the outdoors. But I think they also found the apparently gleeful killing a little alarming, and I was always vague about the dangers of our hunts for fear my parents might have second thoughts about letting me go. I know my mother worried anyway and sometimes took

to her bed until I got back safely. Once or twice my father asked to accompany me, not because he had any interest in shooting, I suspect, but because he thought my mother would feel better if he came along.

Two American agricultural advisors took my father and me out with them one morning. They were country boys, one thin, the other fat, and they couldn't get over their good luck in having been stationed in a land where hunting was so easy and hunting laws so lax. We drove out to a series of stony, broken hills just a few miles from the city. I had my shotgun. The fat hunter lent my father a spare rifle, a .30-06 with a telescopic sight. We shot a partridge or two shortly after sunup, but saw nothing else worth shooting until mid-morning when a placid nilgai appeared at the foot of a scrub-covered hill just off the road. The two hunters urged my father to take a shot at him. He was barely fifty yards away, a big animal, and standing broadside to us. Hard to miss. But my father was as nearsighted then as I am now and could not make him out against the hillside. The watery, magnified image in the scope did not help. "Shoot before he runs," the fat hunter urged. The muzzle moved helplessly over the hill. Finally, just to please the rest of us, I think, my father pulled the trigger. Dust exploded from the slope, yards above the nilgai but close enough to send him lumbering out of sight. I was embarrassed by my father: How could he not even have *seen* him?

A little later, we saw a blackbuck feeding in a mustard field. It was the fat man's turn. He turned off the engine, cradled the rifle on his knee and took a long time aiming. At the sound of the rifle, the buck staggered and fell. We drove close and got down, my father still carrying the rifle.

The buck was trying to get up, to get away. Its back legs scrabbled for purchase, but its front legs were useless. The fat man's bullet had smashed through both his shoulders.

The thin man offered his congratulations. The fat one thanked him. They agreed the horns weren't bad. Not great, but not bad. The buck watched us, mouth open, snorting flecks of blood. More blood was pooling in the dust. Maybe he'd be worth taking to the taxidermist, the thin one suggested. The buck began a low, shuddering bawling, its eyes rolling. It tossed its head and horns from side to side. But which taxidermist? There were two in Delhi, one a good deal more expensive than the other, but also more artistic.

Gripping the barrel of the borrowed rifle with both hands, my father brought the stock down onto the buck's skull. The animal kicked more urgently. He swung the rifle again, high above his head this time, then down as hard as he could. The buck stiffened, then relaxed. The terrible bawling stopped, but the rifle stock had splintered.

The hunters were polite, but full of scorn. The buck had really been dead, they said; it couldn't feel anything. They would have got around to cutting its throat. Besides, the stock had been expensive and would be hard to replace.

As we picked up the dead buck and swung it by its frail legs into the back of the Jeep, my father offered to pay whatever it took to have the rifle repaired. I didn't know what to say to him on the long drive home, but I knew inside myself that he had done what I should have done, that what my friends and I had been doing was wrong.

Not long after that trip, in 1957, I left India. The killing of the blackbuck continued. By 1970 only a few scattered herds survived outside of sanctuaries.

The largest concentration of blackbuck—some twelve thousand animals, I was told upon my return to India last year—now lived near Jodhpur, not under the protection of the forest department but as the fiercely defended charges of a small Hindu sect called the Bishnois, whose fields and villages encircle that medieval desert city. The Bishnois follow the teachings of a 15th Century Hindu guru whom they call Jambaji. There were twenty-nine principles to his creed—the sect's name derives from the Hindi words for twenty and nine, *bis* and *no*—and they included tenets common to ascetics everywhere: no tobacco or alcohol, no cursing or lies, no impure foods. But two of his teachings were unique: All animals were to be considered sacred, but the blackbuck was the most sacred of all; anyone who dared hunt them on Bishnoi lands did so at his own peril. And because green trees offered the antelope shelter from the searing sun, they must never be cut down.

The Bishnois' devotion has rarely been found wanting. When an 18th Century ruler of Jodhpur sent his army to cut down a number of feathery khedaji trees to make way for a royal thoroughfare into his city, the Bishnoi women are said to have barred its way, embracing the trees and warning that they were willing to die rather than have them destroyed. Three hundred and sixty-three Bishnois, most of them women, were killed along with the trees to which they clung.

The women still sacrifice for the welfare of ⟨her⟩ds. Tradition requires that for every ⟨...⟩ water they carry home to their families, a fifth must be brought to fill the communal trough from which the antelope drink on summer evenings. And it is the women who make sure that each village maintains its store of hoarded grain which sustains the antelope in lean times. But at the sound of a shot fired it is the men who come running. Suspected poachers are seized, bound to trees, and beaten senseless. Some years back, an unwitting wildlife photographer had to be rescued from them after he was found aiming what seemed to the Bishnois to be a suspiciously long telephoto lens.

At Jodhpur I was told to call upon a prince of the former ruling family, a hunter-turned-conservationist, my informant assured me, who would be eager to introduce me to the Bishnois and to show me the herds that thrive under their protection. He turned out to be a bald, sinewy little man with a flaring Rajput moustache. His brisk hauteur perfectly suited his new status as a hotel-keeper. He seemed remarkably uninterested in my plans to write about the wildlife of his district until I suggested that I would be happy to pay him for his trouble. At that he brightened a little. Although he was preparing for the wedding of his daughter, he told me, he would be willing to take the time to drive me out into the countryside for the equivalent in rupees of fifty dollars. And he knew where there was a rare white buck. If he managed to show it to me I was to give him an additional "present." I agreed.

The prince—I think it best not to give his name, in light of what happened later—picked me up in his Jeep the following morning. He was a taciturn, even sullen guide at first, answering my questions in grunts and monosyllables as he gripped the wheel. No admiring words I could summon up to say about the flat, shriveled landscape around his city seemed to make him brighten. After twenty mostly silent minutes we turned off the main road and onto the first of a series of rutted, dusty village tracks. Neither they nor his Jeep had improved over the years, and conversation grew still more difficult as I tried to stay in my seat.

I did manage to ask about the Bishnois: Was it true that they still protected the herds? "Yes, yes, of course they do," he said scowling, "though the women are too lazy to bring as much water for them as they once did." But the old story that his royal ancestors had "cut down the bloody trees and the bloody girls with them" was a lie, he said, invented by Congress Party politicians who wanted to make princes look bad in retrospect. He knew politicians, he added. He

had himself represented the district in the legislative assembly: "My people love me." Certainly they seemed deferential. When we stopped for a cup of tea, the villagers crowded around our Jeep. The men wore big loose turbans and locket portraits of Guru Jambaji; the women dressed in burnished reds and oranges, their thin wrists and ankles heavy with hammered silver. When I asked what they would do if they saw someone with a gun near their village, the men all laughed and chopped at their necks with their right hands.

We began to see animals as soon as we left their village. Nilgai trotted heavily away as we clanked through an arid, unplanted area. Delicate chinkara gazelles stopped nibbling at isolated thorn bushes to watch us pass, their edginess betrayed only by the agitated waggling of their downturned tails. When we came out into the green open fields again I felt as if I were back in the midst of some boyhood dream. Blackbuck were everywhere, hundreds of them, chasing one another through the crops, jousting with their spiral horns, dancing right up to the mud walls of the Bishnoi villages. Farmers on camels moved placidly among them; so did bullock carts heaped with fodder and village women carrying water on their heads.

The prince barely slowed. There was no sense in stopping, he said. There were always plenty more animals to see as we circled his city, and he wanted to find the rare white buck that would earn him his additional payment.

I was astonished, and in my astonishment began to tell him of my past: of how many of these animals I had killed, of how wonderful it was to see them again.

"*See* them? What's the use of seeing them?" he said, suddenly alert and enthusiastic. "You're a hunter, you say. So am I. Don't you want to *shoot* them?"

Surely shooting was impossible, a thing of the past, I said.

"Difficult, but not impossible," the prince said, taking my surprise for encouragement and warming to his topic. Laws were made to be broken. True, it would be hard to shoot here. Too open, he said. He could hit a buck with the Jeep if I liked: "No noise." Of course it would cost me. He could arrange a hunt in one of his family's old sanctuaries some distance from Jodhpur, he said, gesturing vaguely toward the faint blue hills that lined the horizon. A relation lived there who was in charge of such things.

What would I like to shoot? A crocodile? A sloth bear? A panther? Sadly there were no tigers in his lands anymore, but anything else

was possible for the right price. We would shoot with a spotlight at night, of course. Five hundred dollars and a few bottles of imported liquor would cover everything, including something for his relative and payments to the local villagers for their silence. For a little more he could even have the skins and heads prepared for me, though I would have to have them smuggled out of India on my own. That should not be a problem, he added. His friends at the Delhi embassies used their diplomatic pouches.

A chinkara buck gazed at us from behind a bush just off the road. The prince stopped the Jeep. "He wouldn't dare stick his head up like that if I had a two-two," he said, taking imaginary aim. "When you come you must bring me one, and plenty of ammunition. And maybe a silencer as well." All I needed to do, his words tumbling now as we drove on, was to send him a telegram saying I was arriving for "the party." We would both know what that meant, and he would have everything ready when he met me at the Jodhpur airport.

It was hot and still now, nearing noon, and the antelope had begun to cluster in the shade of the scattered trees. "There he is," the prince said, wrenching the Jeep off the track and into the fields. The white buck lay alongside two normally colored ones beneath a khedaji tree. His fragile legs were folded decorously beneath him and his horns seemed unusually long. We picked up speed as we rattled through the newly planted mustard. All three animals rose to their feet, staring at the oncoming Jeep. Then they began to skip forward, to run, finally to bound, racing across the fields at right angles to us, making for a high mud wall overgrown with thorns.

We swerved to follow and drove faster. I held on with both hands. The white buck lagged a little behind the others. His left hind leg seemed to have been injured.

"Some village dog's been at him," the prince shouted as the Jeep rose in the air and slammed down again. "Damn it. I knew I should have shot him when I last had the chance. Now someone else will get him." He gunned the motor.

The other two bucks did not even pause at the wall, soaring over it in the sure knowledge that we could never follow. The white buck slowed, then scrambled to his left, head down, horns held flat along his back, running along the wall looking for an opening. We roared closer.

He stumbled, then gathered himself and leaped over the wall, white against the blue sky, floating, already almost like a ghost.

VIII
THE ARTIST AND NATURE

Bull and cow moose at beginning of rut, Alberta.

FOR PURPLE MOUNTAIN MAJESTIES

TEXT BY MARTHA HILL

On a winter evening in 1895 William T. Hornaday, director of the newly founded New York Zoological Society, was hurrying down Fifth Avenue with his wife when he "saw in the brilliantly lighted window of Avery's Art Gallery a big and bold oil painting of unusual size and commanding importance. It looked as if a section with a wild animal in it had been cut out of the Maine woods and framed as an exhibit from the workshop of nature.

"Promptly we crossed the street and parked ourselves in front of the new revelation. One look convinced us that it was something new and different. It was a life-size picture, boldly and confidently painted, of the head and shoulders of a young bull moose going through a tall and dark pine forest. It was signed by a name both new and strange—C. Rungius."

This chance encounter was the most significant event in the career of German-born painter Carl Rungius, for his discovery by Hornaday set him on a path that would make him the best-known and highest-paid wildlife artist of his time. It is fitting that a moose painting launched his career, for of all the animals that Rungius painted, the one he painted most and most liked to paint was the moose. Still, in his sixty-five years of painting and hunting, he came to know and understand intimately the habits of most of North America's big game—elk, deer, mountain goat, bighorn sheep, grizzly—and to portray them in all their wild majesty. No other wildlife painter before or after Rungius has treated his subjects with such reverence and, at the same time, such pure artistry.

Europeans have, for centuries, associated antlered heads with royalty. Sir Edwin Landseer's famous stag, "Monarch of the Glen," was a symbolic portrait of Queen Victoria. To Rungius, the moose was the most majestic member of the deer family, by virtue of its huge antlered head, size, power, and remoteness.

Germany, like England, has nurtured a tradition of animal painting born of an atavistic appreciation of hunting and wilderness. The most famous German wildlife painter was Richard Friese. Like many Germans, Friese and Rungius revered the moose (or "elk" as it is called in Europe) as the symbol of pure wilderness. As a boy growing up outside of Berlin, Rungius knew there was scant hope of ever seeing one in the wild, for they had been hunted virtually out of existence in Europe by the mid-1800s. The few that remained were on the vast private reserves of the nobility and were, therefore, inaccessible.

Carl Rungius greatly admired Friese's moose paintings, which were full of action and drama, and in many of Rungius' own early moose paintings he attempted a similar style. He even gave them such titles as "Before the Battle," "Coming to the Call," "The Challenge," and "Knight Errant." Later on, as he grew more experienced with

moose in the wild, he began to settle for less drama and more majesty, even going so far as to title a painting "His Majesty the Moose." A passionate hunter all his life, Rungius was susceptible to the "machismo" that made the bull moose a favorite quarry for many sportsmen of his day.

Rungius was schooled in the somber Romantic Realism traditional to 19th Century German painting. But he had set his sights on becoming a painter of big game and to be the best he could. He did whatever was necessary to achieve that end, sometimes even at the expense of his family. As his wilderness experience broadened and his technical ability improved, he evolved a style of wildlife portraiture that is unique and—because of his sheer mastery of paint—has not been equaled. And it was his exposure to the American landscape and its big game that provided the necessary inspiration.

Appropriately, it was a moose that brought Rungius to the United States. As a student he had attended the Berlin Academy of Fine Arts; he then served as an apprentice house painter to appease his father, who thought he would starve unless he had a practical trade. He had also fulfilled a military obligation with a year of service he found surprisingly to his liking, partly because it enabled him to paint horses for his fellow

BOTH: GLENBOW MUSEUM, CALGARY, ALBERTA

officers. He returned home to his family out-side Berlin and set up his easel in the barn. There were a few commissions to paint local scenes which brought in a little money, and for amusement, Carl could always hunt small game on the farms nearby. He made frequent visits to the Berlin Zoo to make studies of lions for paintings he planned to hang in the city's public exhibitions.

In the summer of 1894 an invitation to visit the United States arrived from his maternal uncle, Clemens Fulda, a medical doctor in Brooklyn, New York. An avid hunter like his nephew, Dr. Fulda wanted to try moose hunting in Maine. A steamer ticket was enclosed to guarantee his sister's approval. Young Carl set sail immediately for New York, while the town gossiped that his sudden departure must have been caused by some secret family disgrace.

The fall hunt was a failure. Not a moose was seen or heard. Each of the hunters shot a white-tailed deer, but the disappointment prompted Dr. Fulda to ask his nephew to stay another year, for a second attempt in the fall of 1895. It was to prove a significant turn of events.

Rungius didn't mind staying on with his cousins in Brooklyn. The three Fuldas—Carl, Louise, and Harry—were all younger, but they helped make up for the large family he had left in Germany—seven sisters and one brother. As the eldest son, Rungius had been used to ruling the roost. But in the Fulda household he tangled with Louise, eleven years his junior and the darling of her father. Headstrong and smart, she resented this bossy Prussian who challenged her authority.

Rungius set up a studio on the top floor of their brownstone and painted. He reasoned that he could work as well here as in Germany, with such resources nearby as the American Museum of Natural History and the Bronx Zoo. Besides, there was a family friend who had a connection to an art gallery in Manhattan. As Rungius later recalled, "I tried to put my Maine experiences on canvas, but the change of subject was so bewildering that it did not amount to much. One thing I did, though, was paint a life-size moose head from material gathered at the museum and at Sauter's taxidermy shop on William Street." This was the painting that had attracted Hornaday's eye that fateful winter evening in 1895. Rungius was twenty-six.

Hornaday invited Rungius to visit him at

Bugling bull elk in the Wind River Mountains of Wyoming.

175

Ira Dodge, "the first buckskin man I had ever seen," invited Rungius to Wyoming.

the Bronx Zoo. The director was a hunter and collector whose explorations had taken him to many parts of the globe, and the two men found a shared interest in big game that became the foundation of a long friendship and business relationship that altered Rungius' whole life. Later, the zoo would commission a series of big-game paintings for its art gallery. But for the present, Hornaday permitted Rungius to photograph the animals, something otherwise prohibited because the zoo earned money on sales of its postcards. And Hornaday, who enjoyed the role of impresario, took young Rungius under his wing, introducing him to well-to-do colleagues who were naturalists, hunters, conservationists.

Through Hornaday, Rungius met George Bird Grinnell, muckraking conservationist and editor of the weekly *Forest and Stream.*

Rungius was called upon to do illustrations (at ten dollars each) for Grinnell's magazine, and also for *Recreation* magazine, whose editor, George Shields, was another friend of Hornaday's. Shields and Hornaday had founded the Camp Fire Club of America, an exclusive association of men interested in the out-of-doors. And Grinnell had founded, along with Theodore Roosevelt, the Boone and Crockett Club, one of the nation's first sportsmen's groups devoted to the conservation of big game. Rungius was later elected to both of these eminent organizations. Whether he was aware of it at the time, his entry into American society was proceeding on a very high plane.

Another fortuitous meeting helped Rungius resolve to bid his family in Germany a permanent farewell, and to make his home in New York. A few months after his introduction to Hornaday, the First Sportsman's Show was held at Madison Square Garden. Rungius displayed a few of his works, alongside the displays of arms, ammunition, and the latest in outdoor gear. Not at all comfortable with English (Rungius thought it an awful language and resisted learning it), but feeling very much in his element at the show, he struck up a conversation with a western guide, Ira Dodge, the representative of the United States Cartridge Company. Dodge bowled the young foreigner over with his tales of hunting out West. Rungius later recalled, "He was the first buckskin man I had ever seen and a thoroughly Remingtonian figure. He fascinated me very much and we became acquainted. The upshot of this was that, early in the summer, I was on my way to Wyoming with little money and a little short of English."

Traveling in the caboose of a westbound freight, Rungius had no idea what was in store for him. Years later, in a speech he gave to the Camp Fire Club, he described that first trip:

"We got to Opal about 10:00 P.M.; my trunk was dumped in pitch dark into the sagebrush, and when the freight pulled out I could see the lights of the station in the distance. I surely felt alone.

"I stayed with the stationmaster and amused myself with shooting jackrabbits and ducks in the evening. After two days of waiting, Dodge arrived with a four-horse team. Cora was about one hundred miles to the north and we got there in four days. On the way I shot my first antelope.

"Dodge had come the previous year to Wyoming from Montana, where he had been guiding, to look for new hunting grounds and had bought a ranch at Cora. When he came down from Montana late in the fall to take possession, he had a fight with two grizzlies, which crippled him to such an extent that his hunting days were practically over, and a fine territory was mine for the next six years.

"The ranch was located in the rolling prairie foothills, about four miles from the timbered foothills west of Fremont Peak. Antelope were everywhere; elk, deer, sheep, and bear in the mountains. As I had unlimited time, I stayed from June until December. I started with the antelope, working my way gradually into the mountains, until I was thoroughly acquainted with the lay of the land and the habits of the game. Dodge was a good coach.

"Pretty soon I was out with saddle and packhorse, staying away from two to three weeks at a time, and only returning to get new provisions and deposit my trophies and sketches, or to notify the ranch to call for meat. And we lived on the game. The game laws were very liberal; you could kill three head of big game per week to support yourself and your family.

"There were only a few ranches; there was hardly any irrigation, and there were no fences. You could ride anywhere across the country. We had no milk cows, no butter; flour, bacon, beans, dried fruit, and coffee were our staples. My camps were always well concealed. I never had the luxury of a large campfire and built fires only big enough to cook by, afterward to be extinguished, so the game was not disturbed.

"I remember one evening about ten o'clock, I was camped in the last open timber at an altitude of about ten thousand feet, when an old bull elk started bugling not far away. I lay awake for a long while listening to the grandest music I know."

This was a freedom he would never have enjoyed in his homeland, and Rungius immediately appreciated that fact. Years later, an emissary from Hitler tried to persuade Rungius to return to the Fatherland by promising him the opportunity to hunt on

Sow grizzly bear with cubs, Alberta.

Bighorn rams, Alberta.

what had once been the imperial estates. Rungius pointed to the mountains outside his window and said: "This is *my* hunting preserve. And no permission needed."

Rungius went home to Germany in 1896 accompanied by his cousins Carl and Louise. When it came time for them to return to the United States, Rungius packed all his personal belongings and went with them. He had not only lost his heart to the American West, he had also lost it to Louise. It would be another ten years before they married because she insisted, in her independent way, on finishing her education. They were married in June 1907, after she graduated from Columbia with a master's degree so she could teach school. Rungius was thirty-seven. (Two years earlier he had become a U.S. citizen.) They decided not to have children because they were first cousins, a choice neither seemed to regret. Louise's teaching helped to support them while Carl was trying to establish a reputation. To save money, they continued to live with her family.

Rungius was completely devoted to his work, and Louise used to tease her husband that she came fourth in his life, after work, work, and more work. She sometimes resented the long field trips that kept him away for several months, for, having suffered from rheumatic fever as a child, she had a heart condition that prevented her from taking the pack trips. She had tried it on a couple of occasions but found it too rigorous.

During those first summers in Wyoming, Rungius established methods of working in the field that he used throughout his life. Freshly shot specimens would be propped or

Louise and Carl Rungius on the road to Ira Dodge's Wyoming ranch in 1922.

Bull caribou facing off.

181

strung up with ropes into various poses. Then he would sketch them in great detail from many angles. These poses became the reference material for later compositions on canvas. When there were dry spells without game, Rungius made studies of his saddle- and packhorses which would later yield important information about how sunlight reflects off a haired coat or how the shadows of legs standing in sagebrush fall on the plants and ground. This he could easily translate to pronghorns in future paintings.

Forever on the lookout for backgrounds, Rungius constantly painted thumbnail sketches of the countryside in which he hunted. Over the years, he accumulated hundreds of these landscape studies, some gems in their own right. He kept these filed in his studio and referred to them over and over again. Artist Clarence Tillenius once asked Rungius why he continued to do field studies when he had thousands of sketches for reference. Rungius replied, "You have to keep painting outdoors. If you paint outdoor scenes in the studio, your color gets too hot. Only if you paint outdoors do you see the cool, silvery tones that are the true colors of nature."

The other tool Rungius used extensively was the camera. He was rarely without his camera in Wyoming, taking pictures of cowboys in action at roundup time. Most photos were used for general reference, but some of these images he liked well enough to turn them directly into paintings. This practice resulted in canvases unlike his portraits of big game. While the latter tend to be posed and fairly static, the roundup paintings are dynamic and full of action. The photographic reference for moving animals was easy to fall back on, and Rungius continued to take pictures all his life.

The majority of the time, Rungius composed his paintings using a technique known as dynamic symmetry, a system of diagonal lines and division of the canvas into certain proportions. Since most of Rungius' animals were standing still, he relied on diagonals to create linear movement and to keep the eye from being bored.

Working in the field, under time pressure and conditions of changing light, Rungius developed a quick eye and a sure hand. This is especially evident in the thumbnail sketches in oil, executed on the spot, "alla prima" as it is called, or all in one sitting. This did not allow for paint to dry but meant working wet-on-wet. Rungius developed speed and decisiveness with his brushwork. He spent so much time working in this rapid, looser style that it naturally carried over into the studio and onto the larger canvases. This way, he could re-create the spontaneity of his initial vision.

As Rungius' confidence and skill increased, he moved away from the literal, almost photographic work of his early years to a freer, blockier, Cézanne-like style which characterizes his work from the 1920s on. At the same time, he was moving, along with the rest of the art world, away from the dark colors of Realism to the fresh, sunny palette of Impressionism.

But Rungius was also *seeing* more color. In the early years he had spent the fall seasons studying moose in New Brunswick, which had a similar climate to northern Germany's: damp atmosphere with fog and gray skies. The atmosphere in Wyoming, where Rungius spent virtually every summer from 1895 to 1910, was dry. In the Wind River Mountains, which were his favorite haunt in those years, color was easier to perceive in the thinner atmosphere of high altitude, as well as under the drier atmospheric conditions. The most noticeable effect on his palette became evident after the 1920s when he took up residence in the magnificent Canadian Rockies. He had made his first visit to that region in 1910. His first impressions are recorded in a biography by William Schaldach:

"For the first time I felt strongly the urge to paint straight landscape for its own sake. Until then I had considered landscape only as a setting for big-game animals. But the grandeur of the mountains with the marvelous atmospheric conditions in Alberta and consequent color effects changed all that.

"Wyoming is fairly arid in most places and lack of humidity—'atmosphere' to a painter—results in sharp edges, even at a distance, which gives objects a photographic appearance. New Brunswick is heavily forested and lacks variety, hence subject matter for landscape painting is limited. My stay in the Yukon was too short to form an opinion; besides, this area is too remote for regular work. But in Alberta, with its scenic grandeur and its remarkable wealth of big-game species, I felt that I had found at last the land which I had been seeking."

Carl and Louise spent every year from May until October in Banff, returning to New York for the winter. The winters in New York were as important to Rungius as the summers studying wildlife, but for different reasons. Most of his large canvases were done in the New York studio, where he could work intensively without distraction. Those winter months in the city also brought him into contact with other artists and what was going on in the art world.

Buck white-tailed deer.

Years earlier, in 1907, Rungius had joined the Salmagundi Club, a prestigious private fraternity of people in the arts. He quickly made friends with other artists such as Jonas Lie, Bruce Crane, Louis Betts, and Frank Tenney Johnson, another painter enamored of the West. In the early 1900s, such clubs were an important social milieu, providing a place to meet, entertain friends for a drink or a meal, even attend lectures and classes. Rungius liked his scotch, and he loved to play pool. In the club's downstairs billiard room, he could do both, then catch a subway home to Brooklyn from Greenwich Village. Many of his artist friends had studios in lower Manhattan, and Rungius soon moved his studio into the city. Later, during the 1920s, he and Louise moved their living quarters to Manhattan's West 67th Street, where new artists' studios and apartments had been built.

Many of the club's members also belonged to the National Academy of Design, and Rungius was well aware of the importance of being elected to the academy. It was the ultimate stamp of artistic approval in those days, and being able to put the coveted "N.A." (National Academician) after one's name was the surest passport to success.

Rungius always wanted recognition as an artist, not just for his wildlife subjects, but for his ability as a painter. Starting in 1906, he began submitting his work to the fall and spring exhibitions of the National Academy. The first canvas to be accepted by the jury was a moose painting simply entitled "Alaskan Moose." There were very few private galleries in New York in those years, and the academy exhibitions were an important forum for showing work to the public and potential buyers. In 1913 Rungius was elected an associate, and then, seven years later, full academician. In 1921 his painting "Fall Roundup" won first prize and was purchased by the academy. Western subjects enjoyed a wider acceptance than animals, and Rungius was quick to see the value of audience appeal. Four years later, he did win a prize for a moose painting, and thereafter he won awards for both landscapes and animal paintings.

His reputation as an artist now secure,

183

Rungius began to enjoy financial success as well. His paintings were selling for about $1,500–$2,500, and his gallery, Arthur Harlow & Company, sold an average of two per month during the twenties. At this time Rungius also started to do drypoint etchings, mostly of images he had already done on canvas. His draftsmanship was so skillful that he easily learned this difficult medium, which required etching a copper plate with a metal stylus. There was no margin for error. The drypoints were very popular, and over the years he produced more than forty images in editions limited to one hundred. (Many of these were copies of his canvases, only the image is reversed in the printmaking process.) His annual income during those years was the equivalent of about $150,000 today. Rungius was fortunate, too, to be able to work at easel painting, rather than having to supplement his income with magazine illustration, as did his contemporaries Philip Goodwin, Lynn Bogue Hunt, and Frank Ten-

Rungius at a trapper's cabin in the Yukon: He was proud of his hunting trophies.

ney Johnson, all of whom painted wildlife, but only on occasion. Rungius was the first career wildlife artist in this country.

The impetus for this was a commission from his early mentor, Hornaday, to do a series of paintings for the New York Zoological Society on vanishing wildlife. Rungius turned in one canvas a year during the period from 1910 to 1937. Some of the larger animals, the polar bear, mountain goat, sea lion, and brown bear, were done almost life-size, resulting in canvases 66 by 82 inches. For the species he did not know firsthand he had to rely on skins, photos, and the zoo's animals for models.

Rungius produced an impressive series of paintings ranging in style from early ones that were done when he was less familiar with landscapes, and which were characterized by mood and atmosphere, to the later, more colorful, impressionistic ones that made Hornaday apoplectic. An opinionated man of inflexible taste, Hornaday loved the earlier paintings and wrote Rungius a harsh letter deploring his "modernism." The friendship between the two men cooled during the 1920s, but some years later, after Hornaday retired, Louise diplomatically repaired the breach. Rungius merely summed it up by saying that he and Hornaday "looked at art through different binoculars."

From the 1920s on, the Rungiuses spent summers in Banff, a mecca for big-game hunters and others who preferred its mountains for their outdoor recreation. Rungius was a local celebrity, and many hunters found their way to his studio. Even if the hunt had not been successful, they could commission canvas trophies for their walls.

Rungius made sketches and smaller paintings in Banff, but preferred to do the larger canvases back in his New York studio during the winter months when life was quieter and there were fewer social distractions. New York also provided him with clients, many of them men he knew through his various club affiliations. Rungius would casually slip into conversation over drinks that he could turn a photograph of a dead trophy into a living memory to hang on the wall. Many men enjoyed this nostalgic reminder of a great hunt, and their wives often preferred a painting to a mounted head.

The years divided themselves smoothly between Banff and New York until 1933, when the effects of the Depression began to be felt. That year, the Rungiuses gave up the New York studio and wintered in Banff, but this was very hard on Louise, whose health had begun to fail. To escape the worst of the Banff winter, they went to Hawaii in February. The next two winters were spent in southern California with Frank Tenney Johnson and his wife. Rungius was not able to do any wildlife work in either setting, but he and Louise enjoyed the warmer climate.

In 1938 the American Museum of Natural History began making plans for its proposed Hall of North American Mammals, and Rungius was approached to do the background for the Alaskan moose diorama. Rungius, however, had misgivings about the undertaking, as he had no experience with solving the perspective problems created by the curved surfaces of the diorama's back walls. His style was, by now, very loose, and not exactly what the realism of diorama painting required. Persuasion was applied by Wilton Lloyd-Smith, a fellow Boone and Crockett Club member and owner of a Rungius moose painting. Smith was also donating the moose specimens and the funding for the diorama. He decided to invite the artist, along with taxidermist Bob Rockwell, and preparator Fred Mason, to dinner at his estate on Long Island.

Driven out from the city in Smith's limousine, Rungius knew he was being wined and dined for a reason. He secretly poured his drinks into a vase of flowers to keep a clear head for business. He did agree to do the diorama (which included designing the moose battle to be done in taxidermy), but he negotiated a fee of $3,500, more than twice what other contract artists were being paid. However, Rungius was getting that much for his easel paintings by this time, so it was not an exorbitant fee for a painting roughly 40 feet wide by 12 feet high, especially considering that he would also have completed several smaller canvases in the same period of time.

Rungius started work on the diorama in December 1939. By March, the background was nearing completion, and the Rungiuses started making plans to head for Banff in April. This apparently suited the museum staff, since the taxidermy and accessories were to be installed during the summer; when Rungius returned in the fall, the final touches could be added to blend the background to the foreground and the huge glass case could be sealed.

But things started going awry. In May, Louise died suddenly of a heart attack. Then a misunderstanding between Rungius and the museum developed, and the diorama was completed without him. When his biography was published five years later, there was no mention of this major achievement. Whatever the problem was, Rungius chose to

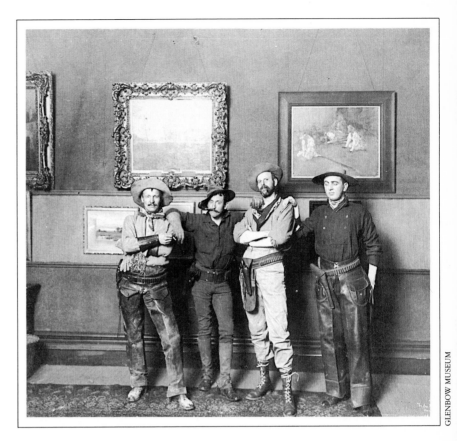

GLENBOW MUSEUM

bury it, perhaps because the whole winter had been one of emotional strain.

It is surprising that in designing the moose diorama Rungius returned to a dramatic theme for wildlife, that of a battle between two prime bulls. His early magazine illustrations had been full of action, although often awkward and overdone. A number of his early easel paintings were devoted to the contest of bull moose (and elk), the ultimate spectacle of machismo in male animals. Only rarely did Rungius paint the female of a species, and then almost always accompanied by a male. Females with young were too sentimental for his clientele. However he once painted a female grizzly with cubs that he probably felt was safe because a sow grizzly protecting her young would elicit respect from any seasoned hunter. Increasingly, his output was devoted to filling commissions from hunters of big game, and his animals became more idealized—immobilized in the gunsight of the reminiscing hunter's eye.

After 1910, with the exception of the paintings of cowboys and ranch life mentioned earlier, very few of his paintings showed animals moving at all. But the romantic vision of wildlife was always there, although it changed from the drama of the wild animal's existence to the power and majesty of the animal glorified by the magnificent alpine surroundings. This vision was

Rungius, at the left, and fellow artists pose in cowboy garb at the Salmagundi Club.

185

every bit as grand as that of Frederic Church or Thomas Moran, whose landscapes of the newly discovered West also used brilliant color to enhance the romantic quality of the subject, a dream embellished in the retelling.

We have very few clues about Rungius' attitude toward his animal subjects and his art. He never discussed art in his correspondence, although he recounted his hunting trophies of the current season with obvious pride. But the passionate hunter was also a dedicated and disciplined painter who worked until his eyesight and aged body gave out on him. Every decision in his life was made with the goal of pursuing what he wanted to do most. As his knowledge of his subjects and their habitats increased, his skills as a painter also increased, and the vision changed from documentary and illustration to one of lyricism. What permeates a Rungius canvas, through his use of color and masterful design, is a reverence for the beauty of the animal in its natural element.

Early in his career, Rungius had discovered the ploy of not dating his work. That way, a prospective buyer could not be prejudiced by a date and think he was getting old material. But even though Rungius rarely dated his work after 1909, it is not too difficult to piece together the development of his style. In the first period, from about 1896 to 1909, he is clearly the German Realist at work, and the highly dramatic compositions are more illustration than fine art. Rungius, in those early years, was preoccupied with events in the lives of his subjects, depicting those of highest dramatic impact, such as the battling of bulls during the rut.

The second period, from 1909 to 1920, marks a developing skill and awareness of landscape, resulting in a thorough integration of technique in which animals and landscapes are handled with similar brushwork and modeling of form. The next decade, when Rungius began his love affair with the Canadian Rockies, shows a remarkable increase of color in his palette and the dominance of landscape.

From the thirties through the fifties Rungius consistently painted with bright color and broad brushwork, reworking old themes over and over. Only in the late paintings, from the mid-forties on, did he show a tendency to abstract the landscape forms of the distant backgrounds. The broadening of his brushwork might be explained, in part, by his ever-decreasing eyesight—a phenomenon that affects many artists as they age. However, Rungius was nearly blind in his right eye most of his life, and it apparently never

Rocky Mountain goats, Alberta.

affected his aim. An excellent marksman, he owned only rifles with open sights.

It was more likely a case of his field-sketch technique creeping into his studio painting. Outdoors he worked rapidly, making decisions of line and color instinctively. The fast, broad brushstrokes on the smaller canvas required a keen insight and sure hand to capture the essence of the subject. It is only natural that this facility would take over his work in the studio.

While his development of style can be deduced from a close study of his work, Rungius' attitude is more difficult to ferret out. He did not "talk shop" with family and friends, by their account, but may have reserved that for his closest colleagues, either in the studio or at his clubs. He did not enjoy a reputation as a mentor to younger artists, yet it seems unlikely that he felt his territory threatened by others. He had carved out a special niche which provided him with great financial success and artistic freedom. He lived exactly as he wished, simply, without the usual trappings that money can buy. He spent little on clothes, preferring the same old buckskin jacket and Mountie hat to a three-piece suit. Even though he did break down and buy an automobile in 1927, he continued to walk into Banff every day to pick up the mail and chat with friends.

Rungius had very little real competition for the big-game market. His friend Frank Tenney Johnson painted some beautiful scenes with wildlife but predominantly stuck to western scenes of cowboys and Indians of the early frontier days. Remington and Russell had begun a tradition of western art that still flourishes today, and many of Rungius' contemporaries found western art more lucrative. The only markets for wildlife painting were the sporting goods manufacturers who needed posters and calendars for advertising, and the magazines and books that dealt with hunting and the out-of-doors. Rungius was able to break away from illustration after about 1910 as a source of needed income and do nothing but easel painting for the rest of his career.

All his life, Rungius lived frugally. Through shrewd investing, he accumulated more than enough to live comfortably. But after Louise's death, he took to sleeping in a sleeping bag so he wouldn't have to make a bed. The trail life was so ingrained in his work that it permeated his daily routine.

Clarence Tillenius is a Canadian wildlife artist two generations younger than Rungius, but as a student bent on learning from the masters he made several pilgrimages to

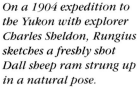

On a 1904 expedition to the Yukon with explorer Charles Sheldon, Rungius sketches a freshly shot Dall sheep ram strung up in a natural pose.

Rungius' studio in Banff, the first in the early 1940s, after Louise's death. Tillenius had heard that Rungius was gruff and unapproachable but found him "open, frank, and genial, though now and then a flash of sarcastic wit directed at some new idiocy of the arty crowd gave evidence that he could be both harsh and cutting if confronted with what he saw as willful stupidity."

His studio was awesome. "Draped over the rafters were horns, antlers, skulls of sheep, elk, deer, moose, together with pelts of wolf and grizzly—all appearing again in the sketches and studies that covered the walls. Rungius was hard at work. On the easel before him was a painting of bighorn rams with several intersecting lines drawn in charcoal across it. Something in the design bothered him, and he was going to take off the paint in the redrawn area and build it up again to the same richness as before.

"On a second easel, in the lofty studio, was a newly laid-in canvas of pronghorn antelopes, and pinned to it were a number of small oil studies of landscape. Stacked on chairs, tables, and every vantage point were pencil studies of sheep and pronghorn seen from many angles and masterfully drawn."

Tillenius had brought a deer painting to show Rungius and get his advice. "When you draw deer antlers," Rungius explained, "you must think of the ribs of a wicker basket—the antlers are like a bowl. Don't think of them separately. Think always of their symmetry—one side must seem the mate of the other."

He went on to criticize the curves of the animal's contours. "Study Reubens," he said, "and see the power he gains by flattening his curves. Use straight strokes wherever you can. Be bold and positive!"

Rungius also had a frequent visitor to his New York studio in later years with whom he discussed his techniques. U.S. Air Force Colonel Richard "Red" Smith had bought one of Rungius' elk paintings and wanted to make the artist's acquaintance. But fearing a rebuff, Smith hesitated to phone him. However, he finally got up the nerve, and Rungius invited him over for a drink. There followed a warm and trusting friendship. Rungius soon allowed Smith to visit him while he was working, and the two would talk about painting. Smith, a bit of a painter himself, admired Rungius' technical abilities. For example, before beginning a canvas many artists will plan the dark-light contrast of the painting by first doing a value study in black and white. Rungius always did his value study in color, and then made changes directly on the canvas. His color instincts were

so sure that he could modulate value by overlaying colors on the canvas rather than mixing them on the palette.

Another technique that Rungius applied brilliantly was the separation of planes in the picture. He understood completely the forms of his elements, a knowledge that made him a good sculptor as well as painter. He could re-create his animals in three dimensions on the canvas by reducing them to planes, bringing the front planes forward with light color and dropping the back planes behind with darker color.

This technique also worked for the landscapes. Planes recede or advance by choice of color and texture. Rungius understood color theory. He knew that warm colors appear close, and cool colors recede. Texture is another tool at the oil painter's disposal. Heavy use of brush and paint will be noticed by the eye and jump forward, whereas a thinly painted, flatter surface will not. Rungius, therefore, used warm colors and textured paint in his foreground areas, and cool, flat surfaces to depict the distance in his pictures.

By the time he was eighty-eight, Rungius had already experienced several strokes which had caused him to become forgetful and disoriented. When he arrived in Banff in 1957, he was met at the train station by his neighbor, Olive Beil. Rungius said, "Olive, what are you doing here in New York?" It took him a few days to finally accept that he was in Banff. When it came time for Rungius to return home, Olive's husband, Charlie (a

Field sketches such as these became references for works on canvas.

Carl Rungius at his easel in Banff in 1953, when he was in his eighties.

sculptor of western subjects), came up with a plan. Rungius had many friends from summer gatherings of the Trail Riders of the Canadian Rockies, an informal group to which he belonged. After Louise's death in 1940, the club became the center of Rungius' social life in the summertime. The Trail Riders came from all over the country, and Charlie Beil made contact with those in every city where the train stopped, to make sure Rungius got safely back on the train. It was his last trip.

In the autumn of 1959 Fred Mason knocked on Rungius' New York studio door to see how he was doing. At first Rungius did not recognize him and refused to unchain the door. Finally, he let him in. On the easel was a painting of pronghorns in progress that the artist was clearly having difficulty with. Rungius put his hand to his chest and said, "I'm all gone inside." Alarmed at his condition, Mason went back to the American Museum's director, who called a doctor. A few days later he read of the artist's death in the newspaper. At age ninety, Carl Rungius had succumbed to a stroke in front of his easel.

The contents of both studios were bought for a fraction of their worth by the Glenbow Foundation in Calgary. Rungius had also sold his house and studio in Banff to them with the understanding that they would become a museum. These were bulldozed to the ground to make way for government housing for park personnel.

His funeral in New York was sparsely attended by a handful of close friends and relatives. His ashes were taken west and scattered over his beloved mountains.

But Rungius left his spirit in his paintings. The artist James McNeill Whistler once observed, "We look at a painting to know the painter; it is his company we are after, not his skill." The very best of Rungius' works impart his love of the wilderness and his admiration for its wild inhabitants. Perhaps the moose, more than any other animal, embodied the reverence Rungius felt for all his subjects. He devoted his life to putting on canvas, with glowing color and design, the majestic surroundings in which they lived, and the grandeur of their rigorous existence, which he spent his life sharing.